The Arctic

MANAGING EDITORS
Amy Bauman
Barbara J. Behm

CONTENT EDITORS
Amanda Barrickman
James I. Clark
Patricia Lantier
Charles P. Milne, Jr.
Katherine C. Noonan
Christine Snyder
Gary Turbak
William M. Vogt
Denise A. Wenger
Harold L. Willis
John Wolf

ASSISTANT EDITORS
Ann Angel
Michelle Dambeck
Barbara Murray
Renee Prink
Andrea J. Schneider

INDEXER
James I. Clark

ART/PRODUCTION
Suzanne Beck, Art Director
Andrew Rupniewski, Production Manager
Eileen Rickey, Typesetter

Library of Congress Number: 88-18337

2   3   4   5   6   7   8   9   0   97   96   95   94   93   92

Library of Congress Cataloging-in-Publication Data

Fornasari, Lorenzo, 1960-
   [Terre artiche. English]
   The Arctic / Lorenzo Fornasari, Renato Massa.

   — (World nature encyclopedia)
   Translation of: Terre artiche.
   Includes index.
   Summary: Describes the geographical features, climate,
and plants and animals of the Arctic with emphasis on their
interrelationship.
   1. Ecology—Arctic regions—Juvenile literature.   2. Biotic
communities—Arctic regions—Juvenile literature.
[1. Ecology—Arctic regions.   2. Biotic communities—Arctic
regions.   3. Arctic regions.]   I. Massa, Renato.   II. Title.
III. Series: Natura nel mondo. English.
   QH84.1.F6613   1988   574.5′0998—dc19   88-18361
   ISBN 0-8172-3325-3

Cover Photo: Doug Allan—OSF—Animals Animals

WORLD NATURE ENCYCLOPEDIA

The Arctic

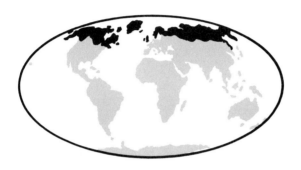

Lorenzo Fornasari
Renato Massa

RAINTREE
STECK-VAUGHN
L I B R A R Y
Austin, Texas

CONTENTS

INTRODUCTION

The arctic lands are rolling green expanses that explode every year with an amazing and spectacular flowering. During the summer months in these vast natural areas, the sun remains almost constantly above the horizon. Despite the almost continuous light, the rays of the sun are oblique. That is, they are inclined, or indirect. The slanted rays of the sun help create the soft tones of color that are one of the dominant features of the faraway lands of the North.

These are the main features of the tundra, a treeless area characterized by a low-growing vegetation, one of the last intact wildernesses on earth. Beyond the tundra lies the vast expanse of the glaciers, which resembles a white desert in appearance. This region is enveloped in darkness for almost half of the year.

Nevertheless, forms of life still manage to survive in this extremely harsh environment. Because of the isolating property of the ice and its capacity to float on the surface of the ocean, environmental conditions are created that en-

able even large animals to survive in this area. The water of the ocean below the ice layer can cool to 23° Fahrenheit (-5° Celsius) without becoming floating ice. Another aid to maintaining life here is the large amount of microscopic algae that is present in the ocean water. This algae is the base of a large food pyramid that includes fish, aquatic birds, seals, walruses, whales, porpoises, and polar bears.

A journey into this vast and haunting land of ice begins at the border of the *taiga*. This is a Russian word used to describe the subarctic evergreen forest of Siberia, Eurasia, and North America.

As one proceeds further north, the differences between the various continents in the Northern Hemisphere start to disappear, ending with the sameness of the polar region. Here the ecology is simplified to the maximum, and all the continents have the same features. The ice is no longer a barrier, but rather a bridge over the ocean between America, Asia, and Europe.

AT THE BORDERS OF THE TAIGA

While climbing a mountain trail, it is possible to notice how the vegetation changes according to the elevation. Forests of broad-leaved trees change to forests of evergreens. Further up, this forest changes to alpine meadows until finally, at the top of the mountain, there are communities of small plants that grow on rocks and glaciers. These changes summarize, on a small scale, the changes that one may observe during a journey from the middle latitudes to the great North.

The Northern Forests

The taiga is the northern belt of the boreal forests (forests of the north temperate region). It is composed primarily of conifer trees, which are particularly adaptable to dryness and cold climates. The taiga also includes such broad-leaved trees as dwarf willows and several species of birch trees that vary according to the geographic areas. It covers a large band of territory, forming a sort of "crown" on the Northern Hemisphere. The taiga extends from 50 to 70 degrees north latitude across northern Europe, the northern territories of Asia, and a large part of Canada.

Generally, this forest appears uniform across all of its vast area. But the single elements that comprise it can change according to the geographic locality. For example, the paper birch of the Canadian taiga takes the place of the white birch of the Eurasian taiga. Similarly, there are many "geographic" versions of almost all the conifer trees. The environmental niche (area within a habitat occupied by an organism) of the northern European larch is occupied by another species of larch in eastern Siberia and by the tamarack in Canada. Different species of pines and firs occupy the same areas in different geographic zones, without changing the general structure of the forest.

Throughout the various geographic areas of the taiga, the main characteristic of all the life forms is their adaptation to the dryness and harshness of the subarctic climate. For a large part of the year, when the temperature is below 32°F (0°C), the plants of the taiga are not able to absorb water from the frozen soil. Therefore, the only species that survive are those that can adapt to these conditions.

The principal adaptations that enable the conifers to withstand the severe climate of the North are the particular needle-shaped leaves and their thick coverings. Both of these features contribute to limiting transpiration (the process of giving off water vapor from the pores of plant leaves)

Preceding pages: A reindeer grazes on the flowering tundra in Norway.

Opposite page: Conifer forests and expanses of water are typical elements of the landscapes in the North. The photograph was taken in the Muddus National Park in Sweden.

The dark, straight trunks of the conifer trees stand out against the curved trunks of the birch trees in the taiga. These birch trees were bent over by the weight of the snows before the trees' leaves had fallen in autumn. Even after the spring thawing has begun, some time will pass before these birches stand straight again.

to a minimum level and to conserving the small amount of available water when the external environment is completely frozen. The epidermis, or outer covering, of the leaf has a mechanical function as well. When water is extremely scarce, the leaves of plants lacking a hard skeletal-like covering will collapse and die from the compaction, or drawing together of their cells. However, the strong needles of the conifers are resistent to withering because of the mechanical support the outer leaf cells provide. Thus, the conifer needles are able to survive and continuously function for several years despite the extremely dry conditions. The stomata (the porelike openings in the leaf that give off and absorb moisture) are recessed below the leaf surface. This position also helps to reduce the evaporation of precious water from the leaves.

A further adaptation of the plants that share these environments is the presence of extensive surface roots. These roots are able to gather water with great efficiency during the short summer season, the only period in which water is abundant. Since the warmer summer temperatures are barely sufficient to thaw the ice layer closest to the surface of the soil, it would be useless for the roots to penetrate any further below this layer.

The tree family with the greatest number of species is the pine family. There are about ninety species of pines. All are characterized by a somewhat round foliage shape, with leaves gathered in clusters of from one to eight needles on the branch tips.

Although under ideal conditions pines can grow to great heights, under extremely harsh conditions several pine species develop low and twisted shapes. There can be thick forests of these shrubs. Examples of this are the extensive forests of Scotch pine in Scotland, which are inhabited by the majestic red deer. The antlers of these animals often exceed the height of the forest in which they live.

The undergrowth of the taiga is sparse. Its trees are scattered, and their foliage is often thin and meager. This is due to the lack of rain and the poor quality of the soil, rather than the lack of available light. The soils are poor because the severe climate restricts the decomposition of dead plant material and the recycling of such plant nutrients as phosphorous and nitrogen.

A bilberry shrub stands out from the undergrowth of a Swedish forest. Many plants of the taiga also grow in the mountain areas of central and southern Europe at altitudes ranging from 3,200 to 6,560 feet (1,000 to 2,000 m). The blueberry and bilberry shrubs are among the most common of these plants. They are the most widespread shrubs in the underbrush of the Scandinavian forests. Other plants of the underbrush are wild roses, junipers, and small birches.

A male crossbill perches on a branch of a conifer tree partially covered by snow. The specialized beak of this seed-eater is particularly adapted to pecking seeds out of pine cones. The beak also helps it to move from branch to branch, as is also the case with the parrot. The diet of the crossbill is closely tied to the production of conifer seeds. When these seeds become scarce, the crossbills will move to other areas. These birds are social animals, and they occasionally gather in small flocks. They are also easily tamed.

The conifers have an efficient method of "regaining" the nutrients from old leaves that are about to fall and be replaced by new ones. As a result, the dead plant material that the conifers drop to the ground is poor in nutrient substances and cannot be readily utilized because of the harsh climate.

The Birds of the Taiga

Every type of animal life in the taiga is either directly or indirectly associated with the conifer trees. This is particularly evident in the case of the birds. The taiga is inhabited by such extraordinary birds as crossbills and pine grosbeaks, both of which feed on pine seeds. These birds have adapted extremely well to the pine tree environment. In fact,

The three species of crossbills found in the forests of northern Europe have different shapes of beaks according to the type of conifer tree that is most common in their areas. *From top to bottom:* The beak of the red crossbill is not as crossed or as powerful as the beaks of the other crossbills. The reason for this is that this bird inhabits primarily white spruce and fir forests. The cones of these trees have large scales that are not tightly closed. Instead, the pine crossbill has a stronger and larger beak. It inhabits pine forests and it must extract seeds from pine cones, which have thicker scales. The white-winged crossbill has a more slender beak. It feeds on the seeds of larches and Norway spruces, which have thinner scales.

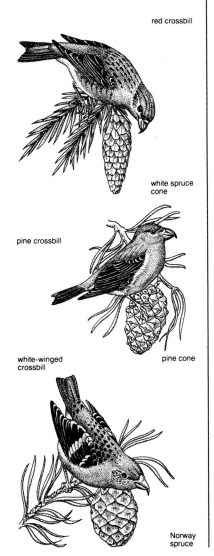

red crossbill

white spruce cone

pine crossbill

white-winged crossbill

pine cone

Norway spruce

their reproductive cycles and their periodic relocations revolve around the ripening of the pine seeds.

The nutcrackers are also closely tied to the availability of pine seeds. There is a Eurasian species of nutcracker as well as a North American species. Since the American nutcracker does not inhabit areas that are as far north as the Eurasian species, it is not considered a true "ecological equivalent" of its Eurasian relative. However, the Siberian jay and the Canada jay are equivalent species. They have adopted a mixed diet and often approach campsites in search of food.

The most typical titmouse species of the northern forests are the Siberian titmouse, which is found in forests from Scandinavia to Alaska, and the similar brown-capped chickadee, which inhabits the taiga of North America from Alaska to Labrador. Many other titmouse species live in the taiga, including the great tit, the black-capped chickadee, and the coal tit. All of these birds eat insects, although pine seeds account for their primary food source.

The willow warbler is one of the most common insect-eating species in Europe. This migrating warbler is so numerous in the taiga that it can probably be considered the most common bird of Scandinavia and Finland. In North America, the Tennessee warbler substitutes for this bird. Although extraordinarily similar to the willow warbler, the Tennessee warbler is classified as belonging to a different family.

The taiga is also inhabited by a group of large woodpeckers. In Europe there is the black woodpecker, and in North America, the pileated woodpecker. Both of these species are associated with mature conifer forests or with mixed forests, where insect larvae are plentiful. These larvae live in the wood of old tree trunks, and they make up the main part of the woodpeckers' diet.

The most characteristic birds of prey in these environments include the hawk owl, which is almost always active during the day, the powerful goshawk, which is the most typical bird of prey of the conifer forests, and the Lapland owl. Despite its name, the Lapland owl is also widespread in North America, where it is known as the great gray owl.

Grouse and Ptarmigans

The birds of prey are not the only large birds of this environment. The taiga also hosts several species of grouse and ptarmigans. These large birds are vegetarian, and they

have adapted to an incredibly sparse diet that consists exclusively of the needles and buds of pine trees and other resinous plants. This diet is possible because of the particular structure of the bird's intestine, which is furnished with two side chambers. The woody fibers and tissues of plants can be completely digested with the help of the beneficial bacteria that live in these chambers. Almost all of the grouse and ptarmigan family show this adaptation.

The geographic distribution of this group of birds roughly corresponds to the area occupied by the taiga. Therefore, the grouse and ptarmigans are limited to the temperate and cold regions of the Northern Hemisphere, where they originated.

The mountain francolin is perhaps the most common of the European species. It is considerably smaller than the mountain pheasant and the capercaillie, which are birds that have the same type of diet and live in the same environment. The mountain francolin is about 16 inches (40 cm) long and is fowl-like in appearance. It is characterized by an abundant black-and-white plumage with shades of gray, reddish brown, and maroon, as well as by a dark band almost at the tip of the tail. The colors of its feathers help camouflage this bird in the surrounding vegetation. The male has a dark spot on the throat as well as a small crest. The coloration of the tail functions as a signaling device. The male displays its tail feathers in open areas during territorial disputes. The feathers are spread and abruptly moved up and down as if they were a fan, while the bird makes a series of whistling noises. This peculiar behavior attracts females and drives away rival males.

The male francolin establishes its territory only in areas where there is a dense underbrush with low-growing vegetation. These conditions are not common in the conifer forests, since the natural decomposition of the needles that have fallen on the ground increases the acidity of the soil. This acidity hinders the development of other species of plants. However, the northern edge of the taiga offers more areas of dense undergrowth. The mountain francolin is regularly found in these habitats, ranging from central and eastern Europe to the Asian coast of the Pacific Ocean.

Other species similar to the mountain francolin are found in the immense Eurasian taiga. Although they occupy the same ecological niche and have the same diets, they inhabit a different area of the taiga. These ecological equivalents are associated with environments having the same

The large outline of an antlered moose stands out among the tangle of vegetation of the muskeg. Adult males reach a height of 6 feet (2 m) at the shoulder and weigh about 1,700 pounds (771 kg). Moose frequent wetlands, where they enter the water for long periods of time to escape the bothersome insect parasites that swarm over the taiga in the summer.

structure as the European taiga. These situations are particularly evident in regions that have a simplified ecology, such as the cold regions of the North.

One of these similar species is the Chinese francolin, which is found in several mountainous provinces of China. In North America, the ruffed grouse substitutes for the mountain francolin. In addition to the dietary similarities, these two birds also resemble each other in the coloration of their plumage.

The Crowned Giants of the Muskeg

There are seasons of the year in which the border between the taiga and the tundra is densely populated by

large animals. The largest of all these animals is the moose, which prefers environments of low, sparse vegetation that look like extensions of the tundra within the forest. Canadians call these environments "muskeg." In the muskeg, the lichens and mosses of the tundra grow alongside thickets of small shrubs.

The muskeg is associated with swamps and bogs, which form an incredible maze between the areas of dense forest. The moose is able to easily move through these bogs because of a particular type of large hoof that prevents the animal from sinking into the mud. The males of this species reach enormous dimensions. An adult can measure almost 10 feet (3 m) in length and 6 feet (2 m) in height at the shoulder. The antlers alone can weigh up to 44 pounds (20 kilograms) and have a width of 6 feet (2 m).

As with all the animals of the deer family, moose antlers are replaced every year. However, it is only after the fifth spring that the antlers begin to take the peculiar form of a massive concave shovel. When the antlers have grown and lost their velvet covering, the male isolates itself and, roaring through the muskeg, begins its search for a female. Unlike the deer, the male moose does not gather a harem of females. The male remains with the same female until she is fertilized. Only after having fertilized the female does the male resume his search for another mating partner. This behavior is similar to the behavior of the roe deer. During the winter, in areas where moose are particularly numerous, they move about in small herds.

In the past, the moose population was considerably reduced because of extensive hunting. Moose were completely eliminated from the western European countries in which they had lived. Today, however, the number of these giants has begun to increase. The total world population of the moose has been estimated at one million animals, with as many as 120,000 moose in Sweden alone. In the last century, the moose was on the verge of extinction there. Fortunately, an effective protection policy has reversed this trend throughout all the northern countries. The policy has been so successful that hunting licenses are currently issued for the controlled hunting of a limited number of animals per year.

Antlered Animals of the North

The winter herds of the moose seem insignificant when compared to the herds of the Eurasian reindeer and the

Thousands of migrating caribou march in a spectacular column. In northern Europe, the entire population of reindeer lives under the control of Lapp shepherds. They watch over and lead the herds to zones that are more suitable for wintering. However, in North America, the caribou still live as wild animals, watched over only by hunters and those responsible for the conservation of nature.

The reindeer is one of the most representative animals of the Nordic territories. Its distribution covers all arctic regions north of Eurasia. *Top:* During the winter, the reindeer migrate south from the tundra to the taiga. They survive by feeding on mosses and lichens. These plants still have substantial amounts of nutrients, having remained "deep-frozen" under the snow cover. The animals reach the plants by digging with the help of their snouts and hooves.

Below: A reindeer hoof is shown in detail. The reindeer's hoof is structured to allow the animal to walk over soft snow.

North American caribou. According to zoologists, these two animals do not belong to different species but make up two different races of the same species. While the reindeer has been domesticated in Europe, in America the caribou has been widely hunted in the wild by native populations.

Like many other hoofed animals that live in environments subject to drastic seasonal changes, the caribou are migratory animals. During autumn, herds of tens of thousands of these animals cross the tundra to reach the taiga, where they can escape the rigors of the northern winter. In late spring, the caribou give birth to their young in the barren lands of Alaska, the Yukon, and the Northwest Territories. In the fall, the numerous reunited families migrate to search for food and shelter among the borderline trees of the vast forest that covers almost half the Canadian territory. In the winter, instead of their basic diet of grasses, they eat buds and twigs of birch trees, poplars, and dwarf willows as well as lichens.

In its reproductive behavior, the caribou differs not only from the numerous species of hoofed animals (in which a male dominates its own group of females) but also from the moose and the roe deer. As soon as mating takes place in the month of September, each male follows its own female, even when the female leaves the group to give birth to its young.

The caribou is perfectly adapted to the type of life it lives in these cold environments. In winter, its coat of hair is long and thick in order to withstand the freezing northerly winds, while in the spring it becomes thinner and darker in color. The animal's wide flat hooves enable it to move with agility over the snow, which is everywhere in the cold season, as well as through the great number of bogs that appear with the thawing in the summer season.

On the Eurasian continent, the reindeer substitutes for the caribou. The reindeer is smaller and has a more variable coat of dark brown hair (like many other domesticated species). An adult male reaches a height of 4 feet (1.2 m) at the shoulder, while some caribou have been known to reach almost 5 feet (1.5 m).

For centuries, the reindeer has been the principal food and clothing resource for the inhabitants of the far northern lands. In the Scandinavian peninsula, the domestication of this animal has become particularly extensive. Practically all these domesticated animals live in a semifree state and their movements are followed by Lapp shepherds. Several

The wolverine, in proportion to its size, is one of the most powerful carnivores existing on the face of the earth.
Top: The wolverine is an able climber that normally drags its prey up trees so it is not disturbed when it is eating. Naturalists have described finding heads of reindeer (whose bodies have been eaten by wolverines) on the branches of conifer trees.

Below: The wolverine marks its territory with both visual and sensory signals, such as the stripping of bark from tree trunks.

of these animals have been introduced into Scotland, where they are now confined to nature reserves.

Like the Lapps, the Samoyedes, Ostyaks, Yakuts, and other Nordic populations still make the maximum possible use of their reindeer herds. These animals supply meat, hides for clothing and tents, wool, milk from which cheese is made, tendons that are made into thread, and bones that are shaped into utensils. Even the antlers of the reindeer are eaten before they become fully grown, and are still cartilage.

Several groups of Eskimos make use of the caribou to a similar extent. However, they do not rear these animals but only hunt them in the wild. The domestication of the reindeer probably originated in Europe with the Lapps. Later, this practice gradually spread across Asia, stopping at the threshold of the American continent. The practice of raising reindeer was introduced into Alaska only at the beginning of this century. It is now used as a food resource by some of the local populations.

The Predators

Humans are not the only predators of the caribou. Herds must defend themselves from packs of wolves that follow them during their long migrations. Once they arrive at the forest, they must also be wary of the lynx and the bears, as well as another unexpected enemy, the wolverine, which is widespread both in Eurasia and in North America.

The wolverine is a small animal. Often, it is no longer than 3 feet (1 m) and weighs at most 60 pounds (27 kg). It has a stout shape and clumsy appearance that remind one of a badger. Despite its size and appearance, the wolverine is surprisingly agile. It moves easily on the snow, running in long jumps, and quickly overtaking its prey. This is possible because of the structure of the wolverine's large paws which keep it from sinking in deep snow. Certainly, the wolverine's strength is also a factor. This small animal is so strong that it can even bring down a moose.

Like the wolf, the wolverine is hated by pretty much all the populations of shepherds and nomadic hunters who consider it a dangerous competitor. Actually, the wolverine feeds mainly on dead animal carcasses. Furthermore, in several areas, the excessive population density of the caribou and reindeer, as artificially maintained by humans, threatens the future of the natural environments through overgrazing.

THE MOVEMENT OF THE GLACIERS

In the past, many large animals lived between the conifer forest and the vast, icy expanses of the arctic lands. These animals had evolved during the glacial periods, adapting as best as possible to the cold climates. At the end of the glaciation period, these animals moved north, following the retreat of the glaciers. The mammoth and the woolly rhinoceros are typical examples. These giant animals, which were covered by thick fur, thrived on the vast steppes of the glaciers. There they roamed alongside reindeer and bison. At that time, however, the environment was much richer than the modern-day tundra.

The Glaciation

The last glaciation dates to the late Pleistocene epoch, between 100,000 and 10,000 years ago. This is known as the "Würm" glaciation in the European region, the "Valdai" glaciation in the Soviet Union, and the "Wisconsin" glaciation on the North American continent. In the coldest stage of this period, the glaciers covered a large part of the land of the Northern Hemisphere with ice layers measuring several miles in thickness. About twenty thousand years ago, the ice reached almost to the fiftieth parallel, burying the greater part of Canada and reaching the latitude of Moscow and Copenhagen.

Many fossils collected between this line and the northern margin of the continents give an idea of the characteristic features and animals of the immense regions facing the glaciers. Mines of extremely interesting evidence have been found in the arc of islands located in the northern part of the Pacific Ocean, between eastern Siberia and the Alaskan coasts.

For some unknown reason, these zones, which were at first free of ice, became covered with ice when the great glacier began to retreat. This glacial process occurred so rapidly that animals and plants were entrapped in the ice. For this reason, they remained perfectly preserved. From this evidence, it is known that shrubs and grasses were much more abundant before the glaciation than they now are in the tundra. They were able to sustain vast herds of large hoofed animals, which in turn furnished food for other animals, such as wolves, lions, and cave bears.

Even many perfectly preserved carcasses of whole mammoths have been found in the glacial deposits. Scientists were able to thoroughly analyze these remains and to attempt some daring experiments. For example, some scien-

Opposite page: This imposing glacier overlooks the conifer forest within Glacier Bay National Park in Alaska. The numerous advancing and retreating glaciers of the Quaternary period have left deep traces on the earth's landscape. This is evident not only in the arctic zones but also in the temperate regions as far south as 40 to 50 degrees latitude north.

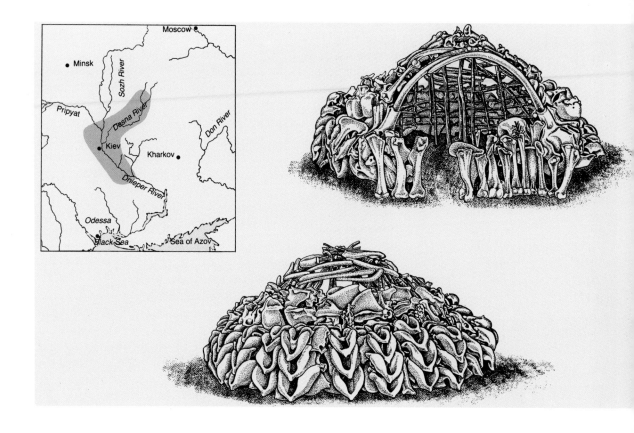

Recent archaeological digs in the plains of central Russia, along the Dnieper River and several of its tributaries (colored area of the map), have uncovered ancient dwellings built with the bones of mammoths. (The two drawings show reconstructions of the entrance and the rear of one of these dwellings.) About fifteen thousand years ago, this region was covered by shrubs and grasses that were characteristic of the steppe vegetation on the outer margin of the glaciers. This steppe was populated by herds of enormous herbivores, such as mammoths *(top right)* and woolly rhinoceroses *(bottom right)*. The populations of hunters and gatherers derived food, clothing, and "construction materials" from the hunting of these animals.

tists analyzed the animals' chromosomes. Chromosomes are the cell parts responsible for determining hereditary traits. The scientists then tried to transplant some of these chromosomes into an elephant's egg cells. These egg cells were then artificially fertilized. In theory, if these experiments are successful, the mammoth could possibly return, with the help of humans, to inhabit the lands of its ancestors.

The Mammoth Hunters

On several occasions, expeditions of Soviet scientists have had the privilege of tasting steaks of freshly-sliced mammoth meat from carcasses that had been frozen ten thousand years ago. Slices of this precious meat were also sent to scientists in other countries, who were thus able to repeat a dining experience of prehistoric people. Humans made great use of mammoth meat in ancient times. This could have been an important factor in the animal's extinction.

In Central Russia, mammoth hunters left numerous traces of their activities buried in the soil of the plains.

These traces were protected over time by loess, which is a fine, powdery soil deposited by the wind in the cold and dry periods of the glacial epoch. Scientists have discovered the remains of about ten small villages that had been built entirely with mammoth bones. The supporting walls of the huts were constructed with skulls, jaw bones, shoulder blades, and long bones of mammoths, and they were probably covered by hides. In just one of these villages, the bones of 150 mammoths were counted.

The hunting of such large and dangerous animals certainly required great cooperation among members of the group. The construction of such complex dwellings, with bone walls weighing up to several tons, indicates that construction labor was overseen in an orderly manner and that the group was not nomadic. These villages, produced with such great labor, were probably used by the hunters as winter homes. During the short summer season, the hunters followed the migrations of the large herbivores. All this suggests that prehistoric people enjoyed a stable social order.

In North America, traces of large bison hunts, dating back nine thousand years, have been found. In these prehistoric Indian hunts, entire herds of bison were driven over cliffs and into other death traps. The hunted animals satisfied the needs of the community with meat, hides for protection against the cold, and bones for making utensils. From the remains of prehistoric camps, archaeologists have learned that bones containing marrow were broken and boiled in holes lined with bison skin and heated by red-hot rocks. The fat that was thus extracted was saved and mixed with berries and dried meat. Afterwards, this mixture was pounded to produce pemmican, a food product prepared and eaten by American Indians even up until recent times.

These nomadic and seminomadic hunters followed the slow retreat of the glaciers northward. Lands that were left behind were taken over—at least in Europe and in central Asia—by other tribes. These tribes began to grow crops and engaged in other activities that would lead to modern civilization. Today, the most genuine remains of the arctic culture can be found among the hunters and fishermen of northeast Asia and among the hunters of the subarctic forests of North America, especially the caribou hunters of the barren lands of central Canada.

Living for long periods in such a harsh environment has produced genetic adaptations in humans as well as the

A herd of musk oxen faces a pack of wolves, arranging themselves in a defensive circle around the young. Because of their formidable horns and their large size, these animals are seldom brought down by predators. Their complex and efficient social organization helps to increase the effectiveness of their passive and active defenses.

obvious cultural adaptations. For example, in all of the populations of the extreme North, the nose has acquired a particularly narrow shape. This adaptation allows the flow of air toward the lungs to heat before it reaches the lungs. Furthermore, these populations generally feature a robust figure. Their bodies are almost stout, with short limbs and a tendency toward obesity, which results from a diet high in animal fats.

A Relic of the Past

In the Eskimo settlements located furthest north, only one large animal is still hunted. This is the musk ox, the only herbivore that can survive so far north. The musk ox is the most ancient of all the hoofed animals and truly looks like a living relic of forgotten ages. It is a colossal, stout beast measuring more than 6 feet (2 m) in length. It resembles a bison, and it is covered with a thick fur so long that it almost touches the ground. Its horns are wide and curved, and they look like enormous ears on the sides of the head.

The diet of the musk ox is even more frugal than that of the reindeer or the caribou. This animal feeds on lichens and mosses and, when possible, grasses and shrubs. Its resistance to the cold is so great that not even the coldest winters will spur it to migrate toward zones with milder temperatures. During the winter season, musk oxen gather in large herds and obtain food by digging in the snow.

In the summer, musk oxen move in small herds composed of females and young that were born at the beginning of spring. These groups are generally accompanied by a single adult male that dominates a harem of females. The males often clash with each other for the possession of the harems. The younger unmated males form small groups of their own.

Whenever predators threaten a herd of musk oxen, the adults form a defensive circle around the young. This circle is difficult to penetrate even for the hungriest of wolves. The adults will not retreat even one step backward, and both males and females effectively use their sharp horns against enemies.

However, these defensive features are not effective against bows and arrows and the more modern weapons of humans. In the last century, entire herds of these animals were shot down with the sole objective of capturing young musk oxen for zoos.

There are three subspecies of musk oxen in the arctic

Despite its common name, the powerful musk ox is classified in a subfamily of wild goats and not in a family of bovines (which includes oxen and cows). The short tail, the shape of the molar teeth, and the structure of the skull are features that make this "ox" a species of gigantic wild goat.

tundra of North America. The most numerous populations are in northern Greenland. In the past, this animal was also found in Europe, as shown by the bone remains discovered in fossil deposits and by numerous cave drawings. Recently, musk oxen have been successfully reintroduced in Norway and the Spitzbergen Islands.

The Continental Erosion

As the continental glaciers began their long retreat northward, large communities of humans and animals began populating areas the ice sheets left behind. Many different traces have been found that suggest the existence of this ice and the forms of life that followed. Some of this evidence belongs to the fields of archaeology, which is the study of past human life and culture, and paleontology, which is the study of fossils. Other evidence, such as the traces of ancient plants and animals that followed the alpine glaciers and later became isolated in the mountain chains, is studied by biogeographers. Biogeographers are

Lake Saimaa extends over the Finnish taiga and is dotted by thousands of islands. The landscape of the "thousand islands" that characterize Finland and Canada is direct evidence of the excavation of the land by continental glaciers in the Pleistocene epoch.

scientists who are concerned with the geographic distribution of plants and animals. Other large traces that have been etched into the land are studied by those interested in geomorphology, which is the science concerned with the forces and events that shape the land surface.

One of the principal properties of glaciers is the sliding movement of the lower layers, which occurs after the gathered ice reaches a certain mass. This slow and constant movement causes the removal of different sizes of rock fragments from the underlying terrain. The action increases the erosive force of the glacier, which continues to widen and reshape the surrounding environment.

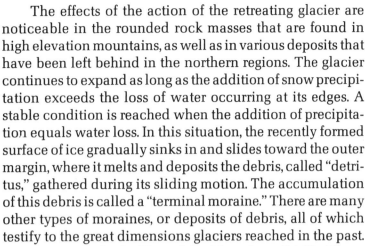

The effects of the action of the retreating glacier are noticeable in the rounded rock masses that are found in high elevation mountains, as well as in various deposits that have been left behind in the northern regions. The glacier continues to expand as long as the addition of snow precipitation exceeds the loss of water occurring at its edges. A stable condition is reached when the addition of precipitation equals water loss. In this situation, the recently formed surface of ice gradually sinks in and slides toward the outer margin, where it melts and deposits the debris, called "detritus," gathered during its sliding motion. The accumulation of this debris is called a "terminal moraine." There are many other types of moraines, or deposits of debris, all of which testify to the great dimensions glaciers reached in the past.

A moraine looks like a thin ridge of small hills. These hills are often found near a basin where the water collects to form characteristic lakes. Other hills can often be found perpendicular to the moraines. These are known as "eskers," and they represent one of the most characteristic aspects of the northernmost regions of the earth. Essentially, eskers are long strips of sediments deposited by the meltwater that flows in tunnels below the glacier. Sometimes the tunnels are several miles long. They can be perfectly straight or branched like streams.

One of the greatest testimonies to the passage of the glaciers and their incredible force is the existence of "regions of a thousand lakes" in all of the northern countries. In these originally flat zones, the moving ice excavated areas of land that offered the least resistance. This process created the characteristic rolling terrains that have later been filled with the waters of thousands of small lakes. From a tourist standpoint, the best-known region of the thousand lakes is in Finland, next to the Soviet Union. In Finland alone, there are more than 55,000 lakes, which are often interconnected and are dotted with small islands. The European lake regions are arranged in a circular fashion around the center of the glacier that once covered Europe. This center is located in the Baltic Sea.

A similar situation exists in North America, where Hudson Bay represents the center of the great glacier. The glaciers of the Quaternary period created the lakes in all the territories of the Canadian shield, from Labrador and Keewatin (in the Northwest Territories) to Minnesota and other northeastern states of the United States. Currently, there are more than 250,000 lakes of this type in Canada.

Additionally, the enormous pressure exerted by the millions of tons of glacier ice determined another impressive phenomenon. A large part of the northern regions has fallen hundreds of feet below sea level because of the compression exerted by the ice of the Pleistocene glaciers. These areas, which include Hudson Bay, the zone of the Great Lakes between Canada and the United States, and the basin of the Baltic Sea, are slowly rising back to their original elevations.

The Greenland Ice Cap

The great and extensive concentrations of ice on the land did not completely disappear after the last glaciation. In the Northern Hemisphere, there still remains an enormous dome of ice over almost 1 million square miles (2 million square kilometers) of Greenland. At its highest point, the Greenland ice cap reaches a thickness of 2 miles (3 km). This gradually slopes toward the coasts, where the thickness of the ice diminishes to several hundred feet. The underlying terrain tends to be more elevated near the coasts. The highest elevations in Greenland are actually found along the sea, where they form a barrier. It is only along the northwestern and eastern coasts that the ice can

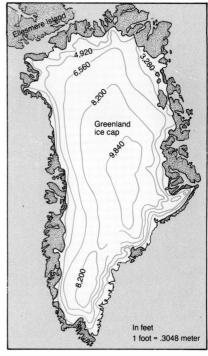

Dwarf larches and anemones predominate in this flowering vegetation of Southern Greenland. Only about 10 percent of this enormous island is not covered with ice, and in this area the only possible form of vegetation is that of a tundra.

actually surmount this barrier.

Almost 90 percent of the entire surface of Greenland is covered by a blanket of ice. This situation, however, has been modified several times since the first Europeans established their settlements on this large island. In the year 1000, Eric the Red described this area as a "green land," probably with the objective of attracting the greatest possible number of settlers. The Norwegian colonies were later submerged by ice at the beginning of a cold phase that lasted until two to three centuries ago.

Toward the end of this cold phase, the glaciers began their slow retreat. This allowed the growth of dwarf vegetation on the tundra and, more recently, of several kinds of trees. Today, the climate is not at all prohibitive. The southern coasts are no colder than the northern parts of the United States. In summer, the temperatures can even reach 86°F (30°C). There are areas of tundra even in the mountains.

THE LIFE OF THE TUNDRA

The traveler who heads north from the temperate zones of the Northern Hemisphere (or south from Australia) will soon notice a singular phenomenon. During the fall and winter, at increasing latitudes, the periods of daylight become shorter and shorter. During the spring and summer, they become longer and longer. Beyond a certain latitude, the shortening of the winter days and the lengthening of the summer days reaches extremes—the winter sun does not rise (and the summer sun does not set) for at least two consecutive days.

The northern line along which this phenomenon begins to occur is found at 66.5 degrees latitude north. This line is called the "Arctic Circle," and it represents the boundary between the north temperate and the north frigid zones.

The Explanation of Day and Night

If the axis of the earth's rotation were perpendicular to the plane of its orbit around the sun, the so-called circle of illumination (the line that divides the illuminated part of the earth from the dark part) would pass through the poles and coincide, at any given moment, with a meridian circle (line of longitude). Thus, all parallels of latitude would be cut into equal parts.

Under these conditions, day and night would each last for periods of twelve hours throughout the year, at any point on the earth's surface. The rays of the sun would always be perpendicular to the earth at the equator. Also, their striking angle and the amount of heat and light reaching the earth would gradually get smaller proceeding in a direction toward either pole. If this were the case, there would be no seasons or seasonal cycles anywhere on earth.

However, since the axis of the earth's rotation is inclined by 66.5 degrees, the circle of illumination does not generally coincide with the meridians. Since the earth's axis is inclined on the plane of its orbit around the sun, it maintains a fixed orientation in relation to the stars. Consequently, during the course of a year, the axis alternates between pointing at the sun, in a direction opposite to the sun, and in all the intermediate positions.

The result of this phenomenon is a period of daylight that varies throughout the year. This variation is greater in the higher degrees of latitude. Beyond the Arctic Circle lies the arctic zone, which has a long period of continuous darkness in winter as well as a long period of continuous light in summer. The duration of these periods ranges from

Opposite page: The summer panorama of the Oxnadalur Valley in Iceland is seen. The gray sky and the flowering of cotton grass, which extends as far as the eye can see, interspersed with small and large pools of water, are perhaps the most representative features of this taiga at the beginning of summer.

This chart shows the revolution of the earth around the sun. In the summer solstice, when the sun is at the zenith of the Tropic of Cancer, the days are longer than the nights in the regions north of the equator. Also, the lands within the Arctic Circle are illuminated for twenty-four hours a day. The exact opposite occurs during the winter solstice. The night becomes longer than the day north of the equator, and the sun never rises in the arctic lands. During the equinoxes, the length of day and night is exactly twelve hours throughout the entire earth.

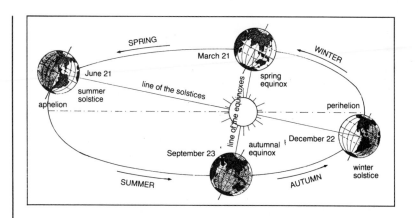

The pale winter sun barely rises over the icy horizon in the sea off the Canadian coast. In the lands of the extreme North, the sun rises only slightly above the horizon during both winter and summer.

forty-eight hours (corresponding to the Arctic Circle) to six months (at least in theory) at the poles. Actually, the arctic "night" at the poles is shortened considerably by the phenomenon of the aurora borealis. Aurora borealis is a phenomenon of light, probably of electrical origin, also known as the "northern lights."

Essentially, beyond the Arctic Circle, darkness dominates from September to March, and the freezing temperatures last at least eight to nine months per year. Once this cold period is over, life explodes for a brief but intense "summer."

When the Cold Expanses Come Alive

The southern limit of the so-called polar climate is quite a distance below the Arctic Circle, and it practically coincides with the northern limit of the forests. Therefore, this climatic region largely coincides with the territories occupied by the tundra, since hardly any trees can withstand temperatures that are always below 50°F (10°C). There, too, precipitation is scarce. It is rare when more than 10 inches (25 cm) falls in a year. Despite this, the sky is often overcast, and the weather conditions are unstable.

This instability is caused by the arctic front, a line along which masses of air coming from the arctic and the southern regions meet. Above the oceans, the impact between the two opposing currents creates centers of low pressure called "cyclones." These cyclones move over the continents, carrying bad weather and air disturbances.

The greatest number of calm days occurs during the winter. At this time it is easy to observe the aurora borealis. However, in the brief summer period, the increase in temperature above 32°F (0°C) causes fog, which does not disappear until the return of freezing temperatures. The water contained in the soil is permanently frozen to a depth of over 984 feet (300 m), and only a thin surface layer of soil is thawed when the sunlight is most intense. The level of the thick frozen layer of soil, the so–called permafrost, varies throughout the year.

The increase in temperature thaws the thin layer that constitutes the only active soil and sustains all animal and plant life of the tundra. This layer is often only a few inches thick. The melted ice gathers in many pools and small lakes where there are depressions in the ground. This water cannot be absorbed by the soil because of the underlying permafrost. Therefore, after a short time, the environment

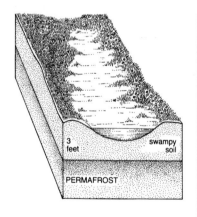

Top: Numerous streams and small lakes are scattered across the green expanses of the Scottish Highlands. The abundance of water in these territories and in the true tundra (which is found north of Scotland) is the result of a permafrost layer in the subsoil (see drawing). This layer is about 3 feet (1 m) below the surface of the ground, and it remains frozen all year. It obstructs the water drainage during the summer, causing the formation of numerous marshes and small lakes.

becomes saturated with humidity, and fog starts to develop. Plants and animals that were essentially absent during the winter come to life during this brief period. Grass stems and carpets of mosses burst forth with color. Shortly thereafter, small, multicolored flowers cover what had been a sterile mat of plants withered by the cold only a few weeks earlier. The motionless and frozen gray plains suddenly become a vast marsh where endless swarms of insects buzz and birds fly, returning punctually from their wintering areas.

The periodic freezing and thawing of the ice contributes to form the landscape of the tundra. Long, uniform fractures are opened in the ground, marking the soil with different polygonal shapes. Lines of rocks are deposited in the cracks separating these vegetation-covered polygons, giving the landscape an unusual type of checkerboard appearance.

Thus, the landscape of the tundra is not flat and monotonous as one might conclude when considering the idea of a cold, treeless plain. Scattered, low-elevation slopes covered with thick vegetation alternate with seasonal bogs and swamps of different sizes. Terraces continually rise and

Lichens are the most numerous plants of the tundra. Each lichen is a complex plant composed of an alga and a fungus. These two plants live in symbiosis, which means that they are beneficial to each other. The fungus gives the plant its water and support on the rocks and soil. The alga produces nutrients from its chlorophyll with the energy of the sunlight (this process is called photosynthesis). Each one of these two organisms reproduces individually. The fungus produces spores, and the algal cells divide asexually. These two new components may eventually combine to form new lichen plants.

sink, taking away any sense of boredom from these vast expanses.

Survival Strategies

The brief summer seasons alternating with long freezing periods make the tundra a harsh environment. In fact, the number of plant and animal species inhabiting the tundra is a thousand times lower than the number of plants and animals that inhabit the tropical forests. The vegetation of the tundra must adapt its life cycle to the limited time available and to the poor environmental conditions of the habitat.

Lichens represent the most common vegetation of the tundra. These are plants composed of algae living in harmony with fungi in a mutually-beneficial relationship called "symbiosis." Lichens can even grow on bare rocks. The oldest plants on the tundra are the mosses. Over the course of the centuries, their growth can form peaty mats reaching a thickness of over ten feet. The flowering plants are forced to postpone their fruiting until the summer after their flowering. No plant having an annual life cycle is able

Below: An ermine wears its winter coat of fur. Although it is found also in central Europe, the ermine is one of the typical carnivores of the arctic lands. It does not migrate south in the winter, and it feeds primarily on such small rodents as shrews and lemmings.

Opposite page: The foot of a ptarmigan *(side and bottom view)* and the foot of a sage grouse are compared. The far northern grouse, such as the ptarmigan, have a thick layer of feathers even on their feet. This makes it easier for them to walk over the snow and to tolerate cold weather.

to survive and reproduce under truly arctic conditions. An annual life cycle is one in which both flowers and seeds are produced within the same year.

The only plants that can survive in the tundra are the various types of perennial plants. These plants have a life span of several years. They alternate the production of flowers with the production of seeds from year to year. Examples of such plants include the fescue grasses, sedges, blueberries, plants of the buckwheat and heath families, yarrows, lady's mantle, and forget-me-nots. Even outside of winter, the temperature is always low, averaging about 39°F (4°C), and the winds are strong and steady. Furthermore, the soil is poor because the breakdown of organic substances is slowed by the constant low temperatures.

To withstand these conditions, all the plants have adopted the smallest possible forms and grow low to the ground. Even the small number of woody species that grow in the far northern regions has adapted to low-growing

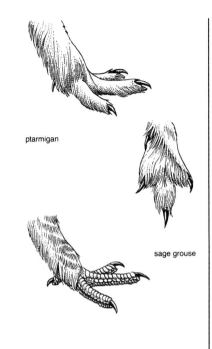

ptarmigan

sage grouse

forms. The dwarf birch and various species of dwarf willow rarely exceed 12 inches (30 cm) in height.

The animals have a certain advantage over the plants because they are able to migrate away from these environments as soon as the climate becomes too harsh. The most remarkable migrating animals are the birds. During the reproductive season, they are the most numerous vertebrate animals of the tundra, and they are present with the greatest number of species.

Only three types of reptiles are found as far north as the margins of the tundra. These are the viviparous lizard and the viper in Europe, and the garter snake on the American continent. These reptiles give birth to offspring that develop within the mother's body. This type of reproduction is called "viviparous." The evolution of this reproductive strategy was developed as a protection for the young during their embryonic period.

The birds and the mammals that live in the tundra all year round have developed thick coats of feathers or fur that completely cover them. In particular, they have a thick isolating layer on their feet. This protects their extremities from heat loss, and it also acts as a sort of "snowshoe," which facilitates their movements on the snow. The majority of these animals have coats that are completely white during the winter season. This holds true for the large as well as the small species, including birds and mammals.

In winter, the fur of the small lemmings and of the varying hares turns white, while the arctic hares remain white throughout the year. The plumage of the two species of ptarmigans that inhabit the tundra is white in the coldest months. Most of the predators are either always white or they become white in the winter. These include the polar bear, the arctic fox, the gyrfalcon, and the snowy owl. The gyrfalcon and the snowy owl are the two birds of prey most commonly associated with the tundra. The adult males of these species are completely white, while the females and the young have a white-and-gray striped plumage. This camouflages them on the ground in the summer, during the delicate period of brooding and hatching. The gyrfalcon has different "phases" of plumage, which range from a pure white to a more or less intense gray color.

The Bird Invasion

At the beginning of spring, birds of all sizes arrive at the numerous small lakes and marshes that dot the tundra

Many species of birds coexist in the limited environment of a pond in the tundra. This is possible because of their different diets and ways of gathering food. *From left to right:* a goose feeds on grasses on dry land; a black-bellied sandpiper and three-toed sandpiper search for food in the mud and in the shallow water near the shore; a greylag goose; a swimming European teal; a widgeon feeds off the bottom; a swan feeds in a manner similar to the surface ducks; a red phalarope feeds on aquatic insects and algae; a greater scaup.

during the favorable season. These marshes are the preferred habitat of the migratory birds. There are more than one hundred species of ducks, geese, swans, and shorebirds that arrive in the tundra at almost the same time and share the available space and food.

The grain-eating geese feed on plants that grow in dry areas, while almost all the species of shorebirds, including the different sizes of plovers and sandpipers, crowd the area between the shores and the first few inches of water. In the water not far from the shore, dipping ducks, such as teals, widgeons, and shovelers, filter the mud off the bottom. At the surface, their tail feathers jut upward in the characteristic position. The swans find their food in a similar manner, but they fish in deeper waters. The diving ducks, such as the greater scaup and the redhead, are found further out in the water, where they swim to the bottom in search of small plants and animals. The small phalaropes, on the other hand, float in the deep water and effortlessly feed on the aquatic larvae that float around them.

The beak is the most important instrument these aquatic birds use to obtain their food. The strong, toothed beak of the goose is used effectively to cut or pull up even the toughest grasses. The swan's beak is just as strong, but it is

used more in the water. The duck's beak is more flexible and sensitive, and the shoveler duck has the most specialized beak of all. The upper and lower parts of its beak are shaped like a spatula. These parts of the beak have blades that are used to filter the material gathered from the bottom of the marsh, even the smallest organic fragments.

The shorebirds have soft, pointed beaks with a large number of nerve endings. This type of beak acts as a perfect organ for unearthing and capturing invertebrate animals, such as worms, which are found in the mud. The length of the beak, as well as the length of the legs, varies from species to species. These two factors determine the different food ranges of the various species of shorebirds. The beak length determines the depth from which food can be gathered, and the leg length determines the distance from the shore the bird can reach.

In the spring, the first bird to reach the tundra is not a duck or a shorebird but a small perching bird, the snow bunting. This bird is almost completely white, and it measures about 6 inches (16 cm). Throughout most of the year, the snow bunting follows mixed flocks of sandpipers, plovers, and other shorebirds of its same size in their migrations. However, when the snow begins to melt in the first days of

41

The snow bunting nests in the far northern regions of North America and Eurasia. It migrates south into the temperate regions during the winter. During the reproductive period, a large part of the plumage of the male is white (as in the photograph) except for the back and parts of the wings and tail, which are almost black. However, the colors of the plumage are duller during the fall and winter. When the winter season arrives, the snow buntings gather in large flocks that fly with a characteristic wavy movement.

May, the snow bunting precedes the shorebirds in the journey northward. There are a few other perching birds that also make this northern migration in the spring. These include the Lapland bunting, the red-throated pipit, the hoary redpoll, the horned lark, the wheatear, and the raven.

During the late spring, all the life of the tundra becomes a frantic rush to complete reproduction . The reproductive cycle must be completed before the freezing weather forces these birds once more to leave this area and fly south. Each species takes advantage of the available time, avoiding rest in order to profit from the long periods of daylight.

While the swans, geese, and ducks generally mate with only one partner, the various species of shorebirds seem to have a wide range of possible types of mating. The small curlews and the sandpipers are monogamous, and both the male and the female cooperate in raising the young. In the three species of phalaropes and in the dotterel, the male (which is less colorful than the female) cares for the eggs and raises the young. Meanwhile, the females of these four species mate with more than one male. Finally, the males of

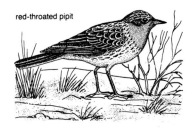

red-throated pipit

wheatear

male

female

dotterel

ruff   female

male

the snipes and ruffs gather in displaying arenas where they mate with as many females as possible. These females hatch and care for their young without male help.

As is the case with all the other animals, the social reproductive systems of the birds act to produce the highest possible number of young. The male of the least sandpiper, which is one of the smallest shorebirds, begins to make its long, trilled call in the first days of June. If it is fortunate, it mates by the middle of the month. After a few days, four green and brown eggs are laid by the female in its shell-shaped nest, which is similar to the nests of all the other shorebirds. From this time on, the female leaves the male to care for the eggs and the young. Just before dedicating itself to caring for the eggs and raising the young, the male attempts to mate once more with another female.

The "free" female may at this time seek out another male with which to mate and lay four more eggs. She may decide to care for these eggs herself. The result of this "free love" is that eventually each male and female adult will end up caring for about four offspring. This may explain why the least sandpiper is so numerous in the extreme north of Europe.

Despite the almost continuous activity of the aquatic birds, they barely have enough time to raise one nesting of young. Before the end of August, the adults molt. By this time, the young have grown their first winter plumage.

As the days grow shorter and the temperature begins to drop rapidly, the young and the adults leave together to migrate south. The skies become filled with the majestic "V" formations of the geese, by the more disordered flocks of ducks, and by small groups of swans, which are sometimes composed only of the mated pairs and their offspring.

The majority of the shorebirds migrate along the coasts, where they search for food along the water's edge. The conditions here are in certain ways similar to the marshes of the tundra. The smallest species gather in flocks numbering into the thousands. These flocks move as a unit, as if the entire group were controlled by a single nervous system. Some of the species characterized by group habits are the black-bellied sandpiper, the three-toed violet sandpiper, and the least sandpiper. These birds provide exceptional opportunities for studying their migratory routes. They are captured in large numbers with various types of traps, and before their release, their legs are marked with bands. This banding makes the birds readily identifiable

A flock of Canada geese flies in the characteristic "V" formation. This species is found over a large area of North America even in summer. There are other species of arctic geese that are not as widespread south of the arctic. These geese are more specialized for living in the arctic lands, and they leave this area only to spend winters in more temperate climates.

when they are trapped in other locations, which may occur several years later.

A Simplified Ecology

In the fall, once the great majority of birds have left, an absolute silence falls over the landscape and the tundra appears completely empty. However, under the continuous blanket of snow, life goes on. Lemmings and ptarmigans dig tunnels through the lowest layer of the snow to reach buried plants. The mantle of snow somewhat protects these plants

from the extreme temperatures. The tunnels are also used by other predators, such as the ermine, which feeds on lemmings and ptarmigans.

The rock ptarmigans are not discouraged by the polar winter. They move about in small groups on the most exposed slopes, where it is easier to dig tunnels through the snow. The ptarmigans are among the most common animals of this environment. But in the economy of the tundra, their role as plant-eaters is relatively minor compared to the lemmings. There are thirteen species of these rodents dis-

Lemmings are the most typical and widespread rodents in the lands of the extreme North. They survive the winters here by feeding on the "deep-frozen" plants. They reach these snow-covered plants by digging a series of tunnels. *From left to right:* collared lemming; bog lemming; Point Barrow brown lemming; wood lemming. The first three are North American species, while the fourth is Eurasian.

tributed along the Arctic Circle. They form the base of a very simple food chain, and they comprise much of the diets of almost all of the predators of the arctic lands.

The various species of lemmings are not all widely distributed over the same areas. Their habitat needs are different, and their areas of geographic distribution almost never overlap. The marsh lemmings, for example, live strictly in marshy areas and wetlands of the North American tundra. In Eurasia, the wood lemmings inhabit marshes and wetlands in the warm season. In the winter season, they take shelter in forests that are thick with mosses.

There are five species of true lemmings that are distributed over well-defined areas of Europe, Asia, and North America. This also holds true for the collared lemming, which is best adapted to a truly extreme Nordic environment. The collared lemming has a patched coat of fur in summer, which turns completely white in winter. This phenomenon is rare among rodents. Other lemmings do not have this feature, nor do the field mice or the ground squirrels, although they are all found in the same environments.

The short nose, the tail, and the very short ears are entirely covered by a thick, heavy fur. As in many other

mammals, the hair follicles (groups of cells from which hair grows) are not single but are united in groups. The primary follicle has a long, rigid hair, and it determines the color of the entire coat. The secondary follicles produce shorter and thinner hairs that are ideal for preventing heat loss from the body.

In adapting to a life in the harsh winter environment, the collared lemmings develop a double claw on the third and fourth toes of the front feet. These special claws are useful for digging in the snow and ice. However, the double claws are lost before the summer season arrives.

None of the lemmings hibernate. The temperatures in these environments are so extreme that an animal so small, even if protected by a thick fur, would not be able to regulate its metabolism if it did hibernate.

Preparations for reproduction begin in the brief arctic spring. If conditions are favorable, three generations of offspring can be produced in a single summer. The reproductive potential of the lemming is very high. A female can give birth to as many as thirteen offspring. A forty-day-old

The Norway lemming is widespread in the tundra of the far North. Lemmings are related to mice and rats. Normally, Norway lemmings live in the mountains. But sometimes, when they increase in numbers, they spread southward into the conifer and birch forests.

female can already give birth to her first batch of offspring. Because of this, the lemmings undergo population explosions at periodic intervals. After these explosions, the tundra literally teems with these chubby little balls of fur, which restlessly move about in all directions.

During this time, the predators also multiply at an unusual rate in these regions. The reproductive success of the rough-legged buzzard, the marsh owl, the snowy owl, and the gyrfalcon is closely related to the greater or lesser abundance of the lemmings. This holds true even though these birds of prey also feed on arctic hares or other animals of the same size.

Lemmings are preyed upon by wolves and even reindeer. To get an idea of the ecological importance of the lemmings, one need only consider that one arctic fox cub requires the food from about four thousand lemmings in a short period of fifteen weeks. In the long run, the high reproductive success of the lemmings cannot be matched by the predators. This high population density results in the extreme reduction of the food supply available to the lemmings. As the food supply diminishes, the lemmings begin

brown bear

wolf

snowy owl

long-tailed jaeger

to die from weakness and hyperactivity caused by the stress of overpopulation. The search for food drives the survivors to spread and move into other areas.

These one-way migrations are well known, especially in the case of the Norwegian lemming. These animals are remembered from the folktale in which large numbers of them were led into the sea, following the Pied Piper of Hamelin. The true situation of the lemmings is less dramatic than the legend. However, in the "years of the lemming" many of these animals migrate to the coasts where they do not hesitate to jump into the ocean, believing that the water is just another small pond of the tundra. Collared lemmings from the Russian tundra occasionally reach the Spitzenberg Islands on natural rafts made of floating ice.

The tendency to migrate is directly related to the availability of food. Each year there are small migrations on a local scale, which are also related to the competition with other species. For example, it is known that many lemmings abandon their territories when these become populated by flocks of geese during the molting period. The large migratory movements of lemmings occur every three or four years. They are usually preceded by a huge increase in the birthrate, and are followed by a sudden drop in the birthrate.

The large population fluctuations of the lemmings and their predators demonstrate the absolute simplicity governing the ecosystem of the tundra. The primary consumers (the rodents) do not have a mechanism for controlling their numbers, such as a competition with other species or a dependence on particular types of food. The only crude method of easing this overpopulation is the mass abandonment of their overgrazed, sterile environments. These barren areas will have new vegetation again only after several years.

The hunting of the lemmings by predators does not have a significant effect in reducing these trends. The sudden drop in the rodent population has a negative effect on the carnivorous animals (secondary consumers). In the course of a summer in which the lemmings are numerous, the arctic foxes and birds of prey may increase their numbers by ten times. They are then faced with a scarce amount of food at the beginning of winter and a dense population of their own species. In these circumstances, the only alternative to starvation is migration. During these times, snowy owls may fly to the United States from the

A varying hare with a white winter coat emerges from its shelter in the snow. The geographic distribution of this species usually does not overlap the geographic distribution of the common European hare. In the few areas where they do overlap, the varying hare lives at higher elevations than the common hare.

Canadian tundra. Others may reach central Europe or even India.

The arctic foxes undertake journeys in search of richer zones. Nevertheless, the majority of these foxes, especially the youngest ones, do not survive to the end of their journey. They are more likely to die of starvation rather than to end up in the game bag of a hunter. The greatest amount of information on the population cycles, at least of the animals of the Canadian Arctic, comes from the statistics kept by the Hudson Bay Company, a fur trading company. The number of foxes harvested shows a periodic, regular trend corresponding to the reproductive cycles of the lemmings, with jumps of three hundred foxes between the worst and

the best years. Similar cycles can be demonstrated for larger-sized animals, for which the same relation between prey and predator exists. An example of this would be the varying hare and the lynx of the taiga.

The varying hare not only varies the color of its fur, which ranges from white to brown during the course of a year, but also the size of its population, which automatically influences the populations of its predators. This animal species does not live exclusively in the taiga. In summer, when its fur darkens, it also inhabits the tundra, occasionally spreading to areas that are quite far north. In the winter, it is possible to find the varying hare at higher elevations, where it feeds on "deep frozen" plants. When plants are quickly frozen, a large part of their nutrients is preserved throughout the winter season.

An Opportunist by Nature

The arctic fox does not enjoy an easy life. Not only must it contend with the bitter climate, but it must also deal with a scarcity of food. Its small size eases some of these problems, but at the same time makes it an easy target for many other predators.

The arctic fox is an excellent example of the so-called Allen's rule. According to this rule, heat loss is reduced in arctic animals by a reduction of the surface areas of their extremities. In the case of the arctic fox, the legs are relatively short, the ears are small, and the tail, covered with thick fur, is not excessively long. Its physical features are just the opposite of those of the desert fox, which has enormous ears and a longer nose to release heat.

The arctic fox is the only canine animal in the world that can change the color of its fur from one season to another. The summer fur is brown on the backside and yellowish on the underside, whereas the winter color is white. This color change to white is not a true molting. Actually, each hair grows out considerably and becomes worn, and later the external, pigmented part flakes off, leaving a completely white color. This phenomenon applies to both the silky and the downy fur of the arctic fox. Because of the appearance of its fur, this animal seems to gradually fade into the snowy landscape to which it has adapted. The true molting of the fur occurs only in spring, when the pigmented fur grows out.

A few individuals of each population of arctic foxes have a strong shade of blue in their furs. This shade is

The arctic fox is pictured with a coat of fur that is typical of the period just before winter. This animal is found only in the regions of the extreme North. Its fur is thicker than that of the common fox, and it is active during both the day and night. The arctic fox generally lives in small groups, whose members share a den dug between the rocks and formed by a system of tunnels. Sometimes these tunnels are quite extensive and include several rooms in which the foxes store the carcasses of hunted prey. This stockpiled food is later eaten during the winter, when live prey is scarce.

desert fox

red fox

arctic fox

The desert fox (of the Sahara), the red fox (of the temperate zones), and the arctic fox are compared. As the temperature of the environment decreases, there is a shortening of the ears and legs. Also the fur becomes longer and thicker. The ears and legs release large amounts of heat to cool the body. A larger surface of ears and legs is advantageous in hot climates.

present both in the winter coat and in the dark summer coat, which has a slate (bluish gray) coloring. This type of "blue fox" is even more sought after by fox hunters and fur traders than the more common white type. People have tried to raise this blue fox in a pure form in captivity since 1885, beginning with wild foxes on several small islands off the coast of Alaska.

The reproduction of this species occurs after spring arrives, females normally giving birth to a dozen cubs. In exceptional cases, this number can reach twenty. The young have about the same low probability of surviving the harsh conditions of the arctic winter. However, the higher the number of cubs in a litter, the greater the chance that one of them will survive until the next reproductive season.

After spending more than three months in the den under the constant care of the mother, the fox cubs come out to face the world. Unfortunately, this coincides with the beginning of the harsh season. The cubs have only a little more than a month to learn everything about survival, before the season of the long, cold polar nights strikes the tundra. As long as the lemmings are an abundant and easy prey, the survival of the cubs is assured. Later it will be necessary for them to learn how to find food in the snow, how to hide, and how to flee from the cold.

In good years, the foxes store thousands of their small prey in natural crevasses and caves, which are used as "food pantries" throughout the winter. In lean years, the food becomes scarce even during the so-called good season. Anything that is edible becomes a precious resource for warding off starvation. They will hunt for birds and crabs and search for dead carcasses of animals that have been killed by larger predators, such as the wolf or the polar bear. During the coldest winters, several foxes live off garbage and thefts of food found around human settlements. On the far coasts of ocean ice, the only possible resource for the fox is to follow the polar bear, hoping to eat its leftovers or even only its dung. This is a dangerous practice for the fox, which must always be wary of falling prey to the bear.

The species of the small white fox manages to survive under any circumstance. Although it is killed off in great numbers by hunger, cold, and humans, each year it survives another winter to reproduce. The white fox shows an amazing ability to adapt to every adverse condition. The zoologists call this adaptability "opportunism."

ON THE COASTS AND IN THE ARCTIC SEAS

Proceeding northward, after the tundra, is the ocean. The lands of the Northern Hemisphere are arranged like a wreath around the pole, the ice pack, and the Arctic Circle. As in all other areas where different environments meet (called "ecotones" by ecologists), the life here is more numerous and varied than that found in the middle of the tundra or in the open sea. The coasts of the continental glaciers are fascinating to discover.

The Coasts

Just as salt water filled the area now known as Hudson Bay in the North American continent, the waters of the Baltic Sea filled the depression left by the Scandinavian ice pack. The waters of the Baltic Sea, however, have a relatively low salinity or salt content.

Despite common origins and a common geographic position with regard to latitude, these two zones show remarkable differences. The differences are mainly of a climatic character. Hudson Bay and the sea facing Baffin Island are almost always covered by a crust of ice, while the Baltic Sea offers conditions that one could almost call Mediterranean. Even the Gulf of Bothnia, the part of the Baltic Sea furthest north, is normally without ice for at least half the year.

Consequently, the vegetation of these two parts of the world is very different. The great Canadian basin opens onto the tundra, which extends east to Ungava Bay and to the northern part of Labrador. The Baltic Sea is surrounded by conifer forests. The Baltic coasts of Denmark, Germany, and Poland are low and sandy. They show the signs of the last glaciation, with a series of eskers that are parallel to the coasts. The fine sand of eskers contains a great amount of a yellowish brown fossil resin known as "amber." This sand is moved to the shores by the sea currents and the wind. It gathers in submerged banks and high dunes that sometimes extend into the forests. At times, the sand surrounds and completely engulfs trees that are taller than 33 feet (10 m). On the other hand, pine trees occasionally colonize the dunes and stabilize them with their root systems, which are able to withstand the force of the wind.

The basis of such an important climatic difference is associated with a warm ocean current called the Gulf Current. More than 3,000 miles (5,000 km) of European coast are affected by this current. It originates in the Caribbean Sea, curving first in a northern direction, and then in a northeast

Opposite page: A colony of puffins is seen on a coastal area in Iceland. The distribution of seabirds is not limited to the arctic zones. Their greater number here is due to the unusual abundance of microscopic algae and small shellfish in the seas of these regions. These are the basic foods of the fishes, which are in turn eaten by the birds.

The map indicates the limit of the permanent ice and the distribution of the warm and cold ocean currents of the arctic region. The boundary of the arctic region is represented by a line (isotherm) that connects locations having a sea level temperature of 50°F (10°C) in July.

direction. It acts to moderate the cold climate as far as the European sector of the Arctic Ocean. Large tracts of the ocean in this area always remain open and free of ice.

However, a cold current originating from the polar region descends along the western coast of the Atlantic Ocean. This current carries with it a large quantity of plankton from the Arctic Ocean. Plankton is a community of microscopic plants and animals that float in water. The plankton represents an important food source for many animals. The cold current lowers the temperature of the water and the surrounding areas of land.

Another branch of this cold, arctic current chills the waters of the Bering Strait, the Bering Sea, and the Sea of Okhotsk, which is north of the Sea of Japan. This cold influence is partially counterbalanced by the effects of the warm Pacific current called "Kuroshivo."

The effects of the ocean currents determine both the productivity of the arctic seas and the extension of the polar ice cap over these seas. In the area of Norway, the southern limit of the ice cap is found at 75 degrees latitude north. In Russia, it extends to the coast below 70 degrees latitude

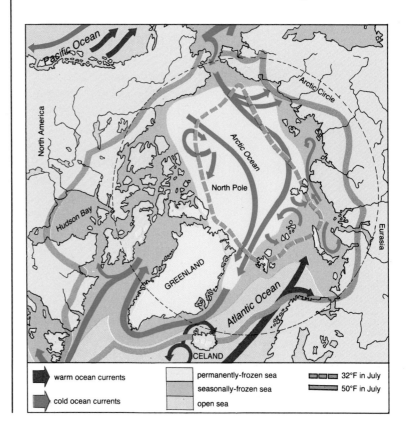

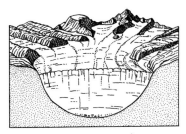

This schematic drawing shows the evolution of a glacial trough. During the maximum phase of glaciation, the characteristic U-shaped valley is filled with ice *(top)*. At the end of the glacial period, the valley bottom is occupied by rivers and lakes *(center)*. If the glacial valley was dug near the coast at a level below that of the sea, then an arm of the sea moves up the valley when the ice retreats *(bottom)*. This process forms a fiord.

north. Between Canada and Greenland, it descends across the Davis Strait almost to a latitude of 60 degrees north. From west to east, the ice extends farther and farther south, and the seas become colder and narrower. East of the Novaya Zemlya Island (northwestern Soviet Union), the Kara Sea and the Laptev Sea are completely frozen, occasionally even throughout the summer. This also is the case of the Siberian Sea and the Chukchi Sea.

The Bering Strait is free of ice, but its waters are cold. A band of tundra extends west and south from the northeastern tip of the Soviet Union, covering the entire Kamchatka Peninsula. This band of tundra follows the outline of the eastern coast of the Soviet Union southward to Sakhalin Island. On the other side of the Pacific Ocean, the tundra extends southward to Kodiak Island, completely covering Alaska. In the Beaufort Sea, the ice almost reaches the land, acting as a natural bridge between the large islands west of Greenland. The northern and eastern coasts of Greenland are surprisingly free of ice throughout the year.

At the border between the large band of tundra and the sea, there are rocky coasts and sloping shores of pebbles and coarse sand. Fiords, which are alpine valleys excavated by glaciers above and below the water's surface, are found in the areas corresponding to the highest mountain chains. The great number of fiords of the mountainous Scandinavian coasts are filled with water from the Norwegian Sea. Sometimes the water in these fiords extends inland as far as 28 miles (46 km) or more.

Along the different coasts, one will always find a small bird that could be called the symbol of these areas. This is the ruddy turnstone, which is a type of shorebird. Although this species is not extremely numerous nor conspicuous, it is widespread over all the shores and cliffs facing the polar ice cap. It nests in isolated territories, not in colonies, and inhabits the arctic areas only in the summer months. The ruddy turnstone feeds on small animals, which it searches for by turning over rocks, algae, and shells in areas near the tide line. At the end of summer, this bird migrates all the way to New Zealand, Australia, and South Africa.

Other birds inhabiting this environment include brants, barnacle geese, loons, old-squaw ducks, and eider ducks. However, the truly dominant birds are the seabirds, such as gulls, terns, and auks, which gather here in enormous colonies.

The arctic tern is one of the birds that nests farthest

The great Columbia glacier is one of the most imposing and spectacular glaciers in Alaska. In the center, a large block of ice is separating from the glacier. This 40-mile- (66 km) long glacier has a surface area of 528 sq. miles (1,370 sq. km). Each year about thirty million tons of ice break off from the glacier (many in the form of icebergs), and the glacier retreats by 10 to 20 yards (9 to 18 m). In the past, there have been different phases of advancement and retreat of this glacier.

Waves roll gently across the characteristic dark coast of basaltic lava near Vik, in Iceland. Unlike all of the other large islands of the arctic seas, Iceland is not a fragment of continental coast. It is actually a piece of ocean floor that has emerged along a line where molten rock (magma) was issuing out of the earth's crust. This occurred at a point where the North American plate collided with the Eurasian plate. This also explains the high level of volcanic activity in this unique land of the North.

north, even as far as the Svalbard Islands. It holds the record for the longest migrations, as it winters in Antarctica. Each bird makes an annual round trip flight of almost 24,855 miles (40,000 km). The arctic tern spends most of its life near both poles, during the seasons when the light is almost constant. This bird experiences the darkness of night only during its spectacular journeys between polar regions.

The Numerous Islands

In the area of the northern seas, the continents are broken up into an endless series of islands of various sizes.

Their origins are different, even though all of them are marked by the same traces left by cold temperatures and sea storms.

The islands of the Baltic Sea have different features in regard to vegetation and rock formations. The southernmost island of Rügen has clay cliffs and mixed forests. Heading northward, one comes across the ancient limestone and phyllites of the islands of Öland, Gotland, Ösel, and Dagö. The phyllite rocks are green, gray, or red rocks similar to slate that have been altered by heat and pressure. Both these and limestone are also present a bit farther north, on the Aland Islands and the islands of Stockholm. However, in these last two island groups, the vegetation is the same as the northernmost tundra, and the soil is granitic. These two island groups include more than thirty thousand islands of all sizes. Their number is increasing due to the effect of a slow, positive *Bradyseism*. This term refers to the movement of the earth's crust from a higher point to a lower point. The area of the Baltic Sea has been undergoing this process since the end of the last glaciation. The Aland Islands resemble a continuously rising dam, which one day may close off the Gulf of Bothnia into an enormous lake.

Denmark is actually an archipelago, an island group composed of 484 islands. There are other islands and island groups further north, in the Norwegian Sea. These islands range from the British Shetland and Orkney Islands near the sixtieth parallel, to Iceland, which has an area of 39,758 sq. miles (103,000 sq. km). Iceland had a volcanic origin, and it is closer to Greenland than it is to Europe. The Norwegian coast is largely broken up into 150,000 islands of all sizes. The Faeroe Islands lie between Iceland, Great Britain, and Scandinavia. They also had a volcanic origin, dating back to the Tertiary period. Iceland is not as old as the Faeroe Islands. It has a large number of volcanoes that are still active, as well as the most extensive land glaciers outside of Greenland.

The Soviet island group of Franz Josef Land lies to the east of the Spitzbergen Islands. The positive effect of the Gulf Current reaches even as far as the Svalbard Islands, which are partially covered by the ice cap only during the winter. The Franz Josef island group, on the other hand, is almost completely covered by ice. Despite the extremely limited amount of exposed land of these islands, seventy species of flowering plants and two hundred species of lichens manage to grow on their soil.

The Steller's sea cow was the largest of the dugongs and manatees. Dugongs and manatees have features that make them similar to seals, as well as to whales and dolphins. The Steller's sea cow had a notable size reaching 26 feet (8 m). This animal, known for its peaceful nature, became extinct only twenty-seven years after its discovery, due to extensive hunting for its meat, fat, and hide.

The twin islands of Novaya Zemlya, located between the Franz Josef Islands and the Eurasian continent, are the first typically arctic islands of a chain that extends eastward. Together with the smaller islands of Kolguyev and Vaygach, Novaya Zemlya represents a northern extension of the Ural Mountains. However, the reliefs (elevations) of these islands have been reduced to a lower plateau that is covered by tundra and plants growing low to the ground. These plants include arctic heath and saxifrage. Several species of low willows grow on the islands from Iceland to the Spitzbergens. However, the arctic willow is found on the Russian islands because it is well adapted to the cold.

Heading in an easterly direction, the islands of Severnaya Zemlya, Taymyr, Schmidt, Solitude, Usakov, Wiese, New Siberia, Wrangel, and numerous other minor islands characterized by ice and sea erosion are encountered.

The islands of St. Lawrence, St. Matthew, and Nunivak are located at the center of the Bering Strait. The Aleutian Islands are found at almost 10 degrees latitude south of these islands. The Aleutian Island chain forms a long arc that extends from the Coast Mountains (in the Northwest Territories, Canada) across the Alaska Peninsula to the Kamchatka Peninsula of the Soviet Union. The Aleutian Islands and the Coast Mountains have a considerable amount of volcanic activity. The Soviet islands of Komandorskiye are located at the western end of this arc of islands.

Even more so than the islands of the Atlantic Ocean, the islands of the North Pacific and the Bering Sea play an important role in the reproduction of marine mammals. It is here that one finds the greatest concentrations of walruses (on the small Pribilof Islands) and the most remarkable aquatic mammal, the sea otter.

Beyond the Beaufort Sea, north of the arctic lowlands of the Northwest Territories, the Canadian territory breaks up into a series of islands. Some of these are larger than Iceland, while others are small and without names. Victoria Island, the Parry Islands, Ellesmere Island, and Baffin Island are some of the better-known islands. Farther south, they close off the opening into Hudson Bay, extending almost to Labrador. These islands can be considered as an enormous expanse of rather sterile tundra that is intersected by a large number of saltwater canals. The northern half of this vast triangle extends almost to Greenland, and it is nearly always covered by ice. The north magnetic pole is found within this area.

Mosses and lichens of extraordinary color are found on the rocks of the coast of Greenland. There are not many animals and plants that can withstand the rigorous conditions of the extreme North. Those few that have adapted are particularly widespread due to a lack of competitors.

Life on the Cliffs

The rock outcroppings are surfaces that are necessary for the survival of numerous different organisms. Many invertebrate animals, such as mussels, barnacles, and bryozoans, which are small aquatic animals that reproduce by budding and form mosslike colonies, live anchored to these rocks. They are "sessile" organisms, which means that they are attached to an object and do not move freely. Sea urchins move among the algae in search of shellfish, while octopuses live in cracks and caverns in the rocks.

The small, single-celled algae that thrive in the first layers of the water represent the basis of marine life. They are the first ring of a food chain, followed by the shellfish and small fish. In turn, these animals are the basis of the diets of the birds and marine mammals. Despite the low water temperatures, many zones are rich with fish. The tissues and blood of these fish have particular substances that act as an "antifreeze."

Above the water layer, which is rich with fish, the cliffs of the coasts and the islands are inhabited by millions of birds that live in colonies swarming with life. There is a

tremendous variety of seabirds, including five different orders. A total of about three hundred species inhabit the arctic lands. Of course, the number of these species is noticeably reduced in the high latitudes of the Arctic Circle.

Essentially, two groups of birds remain. One includes the gulls, terns, auks, shorebirds, and jaegers. The second group includes the albatrosses, fulmars, petrels, shearwaters, and storm petrels. This classification is purely systematic. Using a functional system, one could lump all the strong fliers together, which would include gulls, terns, jaegers, skuas, albatrosses, fulmars, petrels, shearwaters, and storm petrels. Since the auks are not strong fliers, they belong to the second group.

Thus, it is not surprising that the strong flying birds are found in the Southern as well as in the Northern Hemisphere. The auks are strictly limited to the Northern Hemisphere, where they occupy almost the exact position occupied by the penguins in the Southern Hemisphere. This is an almost perfect example of an ecological equivalence. Not only are the general features of these two unrelated bird groups similar, but their ways of living are also. However,

Dovekies are characteristic of the extreme northern areas of the Atlantic Ocean. These small birds are very numerous in certain localities. They are so specialized to a life in cold environments that when there is a rise in temperatures, the colonies farthest south (for example, those in Greenland) will have an immediate drop in numbers.

unlike the penguins, the auks are able to fly. Their wings are very small, and they are skillfully used as fins or paddles in swimming. The great auk, which became extinct in the first half of the nineteenth century, was the only auk that could not fly. Its large size helped protect this species from predators. Unfortunately, this defensive strategy did not prove successful against the senseless greed of humans. In fact, the extensive hunting of this species, even in the most remote lands, caused its disappearance in 1844.

Like the majority of seabirds, the auks reproduce in colonies, which are often mixed. The northernmost species is one of the smallest of the twenty-two species of auks found throughout the world. This auklet, called the "dovekie," barely reaches 8 inches (20 cm) in length. It nests in Greenland, Iceland, the Svalbard Islands, and Novaya Zemlya. Its populations are the most numerous of the arctic birds.

Gulls, Jaegers, and Skuas

Several species of gulls are perfectly adapted to a life on the cold sea. For example, during the winter, the glau-

A colony of murres perches on an Atlantic cliff. These birds look a lot like the Antarctic penguins, having similar shapes and plumage coloring.

A female fulmar tends its offspring. This species is particularly widespread over the region of the arctic seas. At first glance, it appears to resemble a gull, but it is actually closely related to the shearwaters. It follows fishing boats in search of food. Recently it has spread south into new territories as a result of the increase in fishing activities in these areas.

glaucous gull

great
black-backed gull

Sabine's gull

ivory gull

cous gull can be found as far north as the Great Lakes of North America and the coasts of Germany. This bird nests throughout the area of the arctic seas. In the southern part of its distribution, it is found along with the great black-backed gull. This gigantic Atlantic bird is also found as far north as Greenland and Iceland.

The ivory gull breeds at the extreme northern edges of the continents. In winter, it can even be found on the ice pack of the ocean, feeding on food scraps left by polar bears, and sometimes even their dung.

Ross's gull nests in the arctic areas of Asia. During the mating season, its plumage is tinged with pink. This is undoubtedly one of the most attractive gulls as well as one of the least known.

Sabine's gull is a pretty bird with a black head, breeding in the Soviet Union and northern Canada. Occasionally, it lives as a parasite on the colonies of arctic terns, robbing their eggs and newly-hatched young. Sabine's gull is the only gull with a forked tail similar to that of the tern bird. This feature helps it to blend in with the birds on which it preys. On the steepest cliffs, one finds the three-toed gull. Unlike the other gulls closely associated with beaches, this gull is truly an open seabird. The three-toed gull ranges from the coasts of Siberia to the warm waters of the Mediterranean Sea. In America, it winters in the Gulf of Mexico.

The herring gull is found in several zones of the Arctic. Fifteen subspecies are found in the Northern Hemisphere, and almost all of them derive from a common ancestor. The original area of distribution of this primitive ancestor was fragmented by the glaciers of the Pleistocene epoch. This development forced the gull to seek a series of separate refuges. The smaller refuges were later abandoned when the ice retreated. However, by this time the genetic material of the separate populations had developed distinct traits, forming various subspecies.

The most general features of the jaeger and skuas are comparable to those of the gulls. In fact, they look like large, dark-colored gulls with stronger and more robust bodies. Jaegers and skuas are typical of more northern latitudes. There are four species of these birds in the arctic region, including the great skua and the long-tailed jaeger. These birds are considerably more opportunistic than the gulls in their pirating and scavenging. They are also ferocious predators that can attack small mammals, newly-hatched birds, and even adult gulls and auks. They are always ready to rob

the food of other animals, and they also feed on the carcasses of large animals. These birds normally nest far from the sea, in the marshy tundra or in the bogs of the coastal regions, although they always return to the sea during other parts of the year.

Marine Mammals

Many mammals have also developed a high degree of adaptation to the aquatic environment. In fact, some of them can even be said to live an "amphibian type" of life. During the reproductive period, these animals use the shallow coastal areas and floating ice for support. However, they spend most of their lives in the water, especially during the winter. These animals—the seals, sea lions, and walruses— are a specialized group of carnivores (meat-eaters) that inhabit primarily the cold seas of the Arctic and the Antarctic. Other mammals, such as the whales, porpoises, and dolphins, live exclusively in the water. If whales or dolphins are beached, they quickly die from suffocation.

Long ago, the need to solve the problems posed by the

A schematic drawing of the food chain of the Arctic is shown. The life in this environment first of all depends on the energy of the sun. This solar energy produces an abundance of phytoplankton, which are minute, floating aquatic plants. These tiny plants are eaten by the zooplankton, which are tiny, floating aquatic animal organisms. The zooplankton are the main food of many birds and fish. The remaining food debris of the surface falls to the sea bottom, where it is eaten by deep-sea animals.

return to an aquatic life led to the evolution of extreme adaptations in these animals. The adaptations have made the animals extraordinarily different from all the other living mammals. Whales and dolphins are not closely related to seals, sea lions, and walruses, despite several similar adaptations that were developed by both groups. For instance, their bodies have become long and tapered to facilitate their movement through the water by cutting down on friction. Their necks are almost nonexistent, and their heads appear to be united to their trunks. Their feet have gradually become nonfunctional for land movement. Instead, they have been transformed into fins, which are used as rudders and oars. Only the sea lions and fur seals are able to stand up straight and move about on their fins. To move on land, the other seals and walruses must crawl or roll. The hind limbs have completely disappeared in the dolphins and whales, except for remnants of several pelvic bones. The body structures of whales and dolphins are similar to that of fish. They swim by moving their horizontally flattened tails with upward-downward strokes.

The physiological adaptations of the sea mammals are even more surprising. Their muscle tissue is brown colored, due to a very high content of myoglobin (a protein that

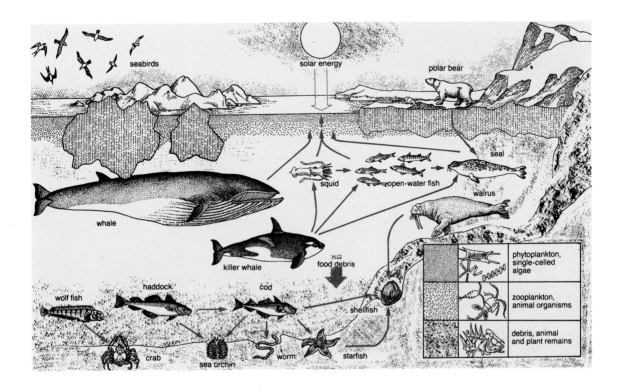

seabirds

solar energy

polar bear

seal

squid

open-water fish

walrus

whale

killer whale

food debris

haddock

cod

shellfish

wolf fish

crab

sea urchin

worm

starfish

phytoplankton, single-celled algae

zooplankton, animal organisms

debris, animal and plant remains

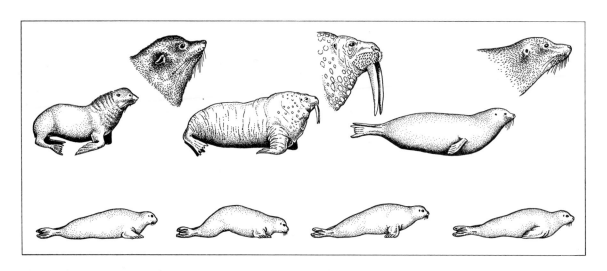

helps the blood transport oxygen). Sea mammals have an extensive blood circulation that is controlled by valve systems. When necessary, these valve systems close off certain body compartments, thus assuring a constant supply of oxygen to the brain.

These animals have also developed modifications in the external breathing organs. The nostrils of the seals, walruses, and sea lions are normally closed by circular muscles. These muscles open only when the animal is on the surface. The nostrils of the whales and dolphins are almost always united to a blowhole that opens at the top of the head. It is from this hole that the whale's famous spouts of water burst out.

To withstand the low temperatures of the arctic seas, all the sea mammals are equipped with a thick layer of fat under the skin. This insulation is so effective that the animals run a higher risk of overheating from excessive muscular activity than from freezing. The heat produced by the body is dispersed to the environment by a system of small blood vessels that run across the layer of fat. Since the skins of these animals can be completely hairless (whales and dolphins) or nearly hairless (seals), they are unable to retain heat. Only the sea lions, fur seals, and newborn seals have a thick fur, which is similar to that of otters.

The mammals that have returned to live in an aquatic environment have also had to solve another important problem. Since water does not transmit light as well as air, at certain depths the water is totally dark. Therefore, these animals are often forced to search for food under conditions of complete darkness. To deal with these conditions, certain marine mammals such as whales and dolphins have developed a "radar" system similar to the system used by bats during the night excursions. This enables them to capture and eat fish, squid, octopus, and shellfish. The seals, sea lions, and walruses feed on shellfish buried in the sand or attached to rocks. The thick whiskers on the sides of their mouths are used to locate the shellfish. These whiskers are particularly noticeable on the bearded seal and the walrus.

About a dozen species of seals and fur seals are found in the seas of the North. The bearded seal is one of the species most closely associated with the arctic environments. This seal can reach a length of almost 10 feet (3 m). During the summer, it inhabits the coasts of the countries that are farthest north. In winter, it is found mainly below the ice pack, where it always keeps a hole open in the ice for

A harp seal moves awkwardly over the ice pack. This species swims with particular agility. It can remain under the water for thirty minutes and dive to a depth of 820 feet (250 m) without difficulty.

breathing. When necessary, this hole is also used when the animal leaves the water to lie on the ice and rest. Because of its habit of lying on the ice for long periods of time, this animal has been labeled "lazy."

The ringed seal, which does not measure more than 5 feet (1.5 m), has similar habits. Each ringed seal uses several holes in the ice. Usually one of these is the "preferred" hole, and the seal defends it as its own territory. In spring, these seals shed their fur near these holes, and the females give birth in a den dug in the snow.

The ringed seal is perhaps the most numerous seal, since it reproduces in dens that are hard to find. Moreover, it does not live in colonies. Seals that live in colonies are more easily hunted in large numbers, and their population has been estimated at more than five million, divided into numerous subspecies. Some of these subspecies are limited to the Baltic Sea and to the lakes of northeastern Europe and Finland. These "relic" populations remained in these areas after the retreat of the great Pleistocene glacier. The subspecies never leave their reproductive territories.

However, there are other seals that make long migrations along the margins of the ice pack, where they stay long

A walrus family rests calmly on top of a drifting sheet of ice. The walrus was extensively hunted in the past for its enormous quantity of fat and the ivory of its tusks. Presently, only Eskimos are permitted to hunt this animal, as they depend on it for food.

Following pages: A group of humpback whales makes spectacular leaps out of the water. Commercial whale hunting is facing strong opposition by the public. This hunting is protested not only because of the danger of extinction for many species, but also because the killing of such intelligent animals has now become unacceptable to a growing number of people.

enough to shed and reproduce. This behavior is characteristic of the hooded seals, which reunite in the summer months in the Denmark Strait between Greenland and Iceland. Another numerous species, the harp seal, follows this same route. This seal is well known for the silky white fur of its young. There are three known populations of the harp seal that migrate to reproduce in different zones. These zones are the Gulf of St. Lawrence, the Greenland Sea, the waters of the Baltic Sea, and the northernmost European islands.

In the extreme North Pacific, the harp seal is replaced by a similar but smaller species called the "ribbon seal." The harbor seal and the gray seal have less localized distributions, and they also inhabit the coasts of the temperate regions. Another species which is limited to the cold waters of the Bering Sea is the impressive Steller sea lion. This animal can exceed 11 feet (3.5 m) in length and is more closely related to the fur seals than the common seals. It inhabits the same area as the northern fur seal, which is widely hunted for its fur.

However, the walrus is the most characteristic and symbolic of all these animals. This 1,985-pound (900-

kg) giant instantly evokes the image of the arctic ice. The walrus is not as widespread as it once was in the past. Only several tens of thousands of these animals remain. They populate three separate geographic areas in the Pacific, the Laptev Sea, and the Atlantic. The walrus is valued for its fat and its ivory tusks. For this reason, an increasing number of commercial and exploratory hunting expeditions have been carried out over the last century. This has caused the fragmented distribution of the animal.

Because of an international agreement, the walrus can now be hunted only by native peoples of the arctic lands. These people depend on this animal as a major food source. The fate of the walrus has also befallen many of the large whales. The right whales and the finback whales can be considered extinct from a commercial point of view. In other words, they have become so rare that their hunting is not economically profitable.

The smaller whales have not been as widely hunted by humans, although several of these animals make up a regular part of the diet of native tribes. The meat of two particular species, the beluga and the narwhale, is widely consumed. These species do not exceed 16 feet (5 m) in length, and they generally inhabit the waters near the ice pack. During the winter, they move south, sometimes swimming considerable distances up rivers.

The narwhale male is famous for the development of a single tooth which, with time, takes the shape of a spiral horn. This tooth extends over 6 feet (2 m) past the snout of the animal. The beluga is known for the pure white color that characterizes the adults. The forehead of the beluga is quite large. Together with the snout, it forms a surface perpendicular to the length of the body. This characteristic is probably related to the ability of this whale to receive sound waves generated by other animals in the water. Under the thick, elastic skin and a thick layer of fat, the beluga whale has a large bubble of oil. This oil bubble's form can be modified and is perhaps related to the sonar system of the animal. The layer of fat under the skin is much softer than in the other whales. This fat is particularly valued as food by Eskimos, who call it "mukluk." Large pieces of this prized food are often hung to dry on scaffolds near their summer huts, outside of the reach of foxes and sled dogs.

THE LARGE PREDATORS OF THE SEAS

The coastal region is rich with life. This abundance of animals offers enough food for considerable numbers of specialized predators. Among them, the sea eagle and the killer whale deserve particular attention.

Sea Eagles

Sea eagles are large birds that are adapted to a life along the coasts, lakes, marshes, and streams. They feed on a large number of prey, including fish, birds, mammals, reptiles, and amphibians. Sea eagles capture live prey, but they also feed on carcasses.

Eight species of sea eagles are found throughout the world, and they all have similar life-styles. Only three species live in the arctic areas. These are the gray sea eagle of Eurasia, the bald eagle of North America, and the Steller's sea eagle of eastern Siberia and northern Japan.

The Steller's sea eagle is the largest and most spectacular of all. Its plumage is almost completely black except for the shoulders, forehead, and tail, which are white. This bird has an enormous beak, comparable to that of the legendary roc, and an almost incredible body mass. Some females can reach a weight of 40 pounds (18 kg). This is truly amazing if one considers that the largest Eurasian sea eagles weigh no more than 16 pounds (7.5 kg), and the bald eagle is even smaller. These comparisons are true only of the female sea eagles, which normally weigh twice as much as the males.

The sea eagle has a disproportionately large beak. It is much larger than the beak of the golden eagle, even though the sea eagle eats less food. Sea eagles feed on herring, cod, catfish, gulls, cormorants, eider ducks, field mice, rabbits, hares, and even small reindeer and roe deer. They also feed on beached or floating carcasses of whales and seals. Sea eagles often rob other birds of prey of their captured food, especially the osprey. Occasionally, they even attack lambs or small goats.

Because of their habit of attacking domestic livestock, many sea eagles have been killed in Europe and in North America. For example, in Norway in the second half of the nineteenth century, a bounty was paid for every sea eagle killed. In just one year 1,500 of these birds were killed in Norway, and more than 90,000 eagles were turned in during the second half of the last century. This is an enormous number, even for a region with numerous natural habitats along the coast and on the countless islands.

It is not surprising that the bounties that were offered

Opposite page: The gray sea eagle is one of the greatest predators of Eurasia. It was exterminated throughout most of Europe because people mistakenly believed that it preyed extensively on livestock. Recently it has been reintroduced into Scotland. There are also a limited number of pairs of this species on the coasts of Norway.

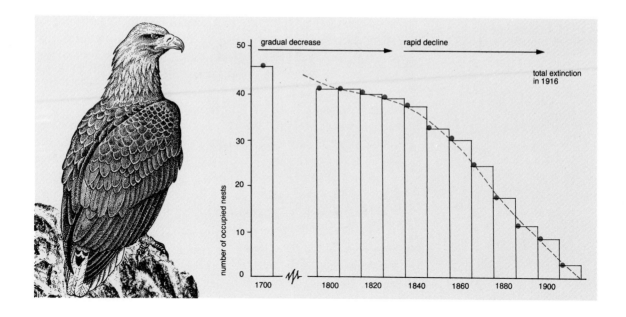

The graph shows the dramatic decline of the population of the gray sea eagle *(left)* in Great Britain. At the beginning of the nineteenth century, forty-five nesting pairs were counted over all the British territory. The species did not suffer a steep decline until 1840. During the second half of the nineteenth century, the gray sea eagle was widely killed by people, causing its eventual extinction in 1916.

decreased with time, since the sea eagles became scarce. This practice, however, continued until 1932, when the national bounty system was abolished. Unfortunately, this did not protect these birds of prey from the new bounties offered by local authorities and hunting associations.

Today, the total population of sea eagles in Norway is estimated at 450 pairs. Fortunately, the population has been increasing since 1968, when the sea eagle finally became a protected species. The populations of sea eagles in other countries are less fortunate. Currently, there are only 18 pairs of these birds in Finland and 5 pairs in West Germany. They became extinct in Scotland in 1916 after their population showed a gradual decline over a period of approximately one hundred years, due to widespread killing.

An attempt to reintroduce the sea eagle on Rum Island (in northwestern Scotland) was begun in 1975. Under the direction of John Love, this program aimed at releasing fifty young eagles that had been taken from Norway at a very young age, over a period of ten years. Capturing a young eagle from nests having at least two offspring is not harmful to the population, since the larger bird of the nest normally kills the other offspring in the wild.

The first successful reproduction in the wild of released birds occurred in 1985. In the meantime, the sea eagles have begun to spread to other areas of Scotland.

A similar situation applies to the bald eagle, the symbol

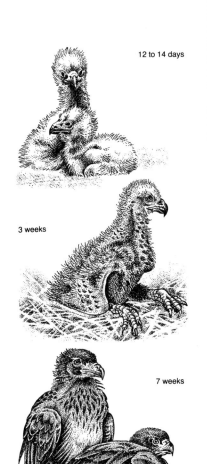

Newborn sea eagles are shown in different stages of development. *From top to bottom:* At two weeks, at three weeks, at seven weeks. In the last phase, the young eagles are completely covered by feathers. But they remain in the nest until the age of about ten weeks, strengthening their wings and preparing for their first flight.

12 to 14 days

3 weeks

7 weeks

of the United States. In the first half of this century, more than one hundred thousand of these splendid birds were killed in the United States alone. Until 1940, each bald eagle killed brought a bounty of one dollar. The hunting of the bald eagle was finally prohibited. Unfortunately, by the time the law became effective, the number of bald eagles had been reduced to fewer than one thousand birds.

The most ridiculous aspect of this situation is that the sea eagle feeds primarily on carcasses or prey stolen from other birds of prey. The bald eagle normally captures salmon after they have reproduced. At this time, the salmon have used up all their energy and swim into shallow water to die. Therefore, the anti-eagle campaigns never had any justification, not even from an economic standpoint.

Sea eagles build enormous nests, which in some cases can weigh up to several hundred pounds, as the result of a series of additions over a period of many years. Each year, the mated pair may add a layer of up to 3 feet (1 m) in thickness. The female normally lays one or two eggs (rarely will three eggs be laid), and usually only one young survives to the flying stage. The young hatch after forty days. They weigh a little more than 3.5 ounces (100 grams), and they are born blind and without hair. After the fourth week, they look like balls of downy feathers. But after ten weeks, they are completely developed and ready to make their first flight. At this time, they weigh between 9 and 13 pounds (4 and 6 kg), and their plumage is still a uniform dark brown, without the characteristic white tail. In central Europe, these young eagles are ready to fly at the end of April. In Norway, they do not leave the nest before the middle of June. In the Soviet area of the White Sea, the first flights do not occur until August.

The Killer Whale

The animals of the sea must always be on guard against the danger of flying predators over the water, but their most dangerous enemy is a predator that lives in the water. This is the killer whale, an animal that can reach a length of about 29 feet (9 m). It is the largest member of the dolphin family, as well as the most powerful predator that exists on earth.

During the course of evolution, there have been other instances of a superpredator evolving within a group of related animal species. These superpredators prey on other species. There are spiders that feed on other spiders, snakes

The killer whale has a huge appetite. It has twenty large conical teeth on each side of its jaw. These can grab onto any type of prey, including slippery sea snails. It is a rapid swimmer, reaching a speed of 27 miles (45 km) per hour. It can descend to depths of 3,200 feet (1,000 m) without difficulty and remain submerged for twenty minutes. It normally moves in groups of from five to fifty individuals, presumably composed of different family groups.

that feed on other snakes, and so forth. Likewise, the killer whale is a sea mammal that feeds on other sea mammals. It is a dolphin that feeds on other dolphins.

The males reach a length of 29 feet (9 m), whereas the females generally do not exceed 16 feet (5 m). Occasionally, the killer whale preys on larger whales. This animal is armed with large and powerful conical teeth on each side of its jaws. It also has an extraordinary intelligence. The killer whales have sometimes been called the "wolves of the ocean," since they attack their largest prey in packs. With a coordinated effort, they attach themselves to the tail, fins, and head of this larger prey. The killer whale is found in

the seas throughout the world. However, the highest densities of its population are found in the polar seas. Like all the other superpredators, the killer whales are not common in any area of their distribution.

If a group of killer whales captures a whale, they eat its tongue and head, a feat requiring the coordinated action of many killer whales. Generally, they move about in groups of two to five individuals, feeding on such smaller prey as dolphins, porpoises, seals, and sea lions. These smaller prey are swallowed whole. On several occasions, the remains of more than twenty porpoises and seals have been found in a killer whale's stomach.

Instruments such as these are used by the Eskimos for hunting and fishing in the open sea. *From left to right:* harpoon with bobber, fishing arrow, and seal spear. The small-scale hunting practiced by the Eskimos does not have a damaging effect on the populations of arctic animals. This type of hunting is different from the commercial hunting that utilizes modern instruments, which sometimes threatens the extinction of the hunted species.

Killer whales demonstrate their considerable intelligence while hunting for seals. On those occasions, they break apart blocks of floating ice from below, which causes the seals on top of the ice to fall into the water, where they are eaten. Despite their power, it appears that killer whales have never attacked humans. The few killer whales living in captivity have always been friendly and affectionate with their keepers.

The Money-making Predator

The poor soils and the harsh climates of the far North make the cultivation of plants for human consumption or feed for livestock virtually impossible. Consequently, people in these areas must live almost exclusively on hunting and fishing. The adaptation of humans to this life-style has been going on for many thousands of years. The isolated human populations of the North have perfectly integrated into the natural balance. They hunt on a small scale, which does not produce a negative effect on the animal populations.

The coastal Eskimos are the most numerous of these peoples, and they take advantage of the natural abundance of certain resources according to the seasonal cycles of the resources. For example, during the winter they live off seals that are hunted on the ice pack. Dogs sniff out the breathing holes of the seals, and the hunters patiently wait outside these holes for the animals to appear from the water.

At the end of the winter, when the sea ice begins to open, Eskimos hunt seals and walruses in the open arms of the sea and on ice rafts where these animals gather to warm themselves in the sun. The walruses are the most desirable prey since their large size provides abundant supplies of meat. The partially digested shellfish that are usually found in their stomachs are considered a delicacy, and Eskimos eat them almost immediately.

To capture these sea mammals, the hunters use carefully constructed harpoons. Each harpoon is made of a wooden pole, a piece of ivory joined to the pole with a central piece and several laces, and a head that is attached to the ivory piece through a hole at its base. The tip of the head carries a point that used to be made of flint. However, when Eskimos began to trade with white settlers, they acquired iron, and replaced the flint tip with an iron one. A long gut cord runs from the head of the harpoon to the pole, which in turn is tied to the hunter. Sometimes an air-filled

An Eskimo fishes through a hole in the ice pack.

pouch made of sealskin or other material is tied to the end of the cord. This functions as a sort of bobber.

When Eskimos strike an animal in the open sea, the hook-shaped head of the harpoon remains inside the flesh of the animal and the bobber signals the position of the cord and the harpoon. Eskimos often use a special device to increase the force with which the harpoon is launched. This is a type of bar that acts as an extended arm. The use of firearms in place of the harpoon leads to the loss of the animal, which dies on the sea bottom and cannot be retrieved.

Toward May, when the thawing is complete, the Eskimos also hunt for whales and dolphins in the open sea. This hunting takes place over a wide area extending to the mouths of the Mackenzie River on one side and Hudson Bay and Smith Strait on the other. In the spring months, the Eskimos also hunt the polar bear and the musk ox. Toward the middle of the summer, they begin to hunt the caribou that have returned from their wintering areas.

While hunting by Eskimos is done solely for survival,

that done by fur traders is motivated by economic profit. Fur traders kill the young Greenland seals during the first few weeks of their lives, when the little cubs are covered by a soft, white fur. At the age of one month, before the young seals enter the water for the first time, this fur changes into an economically useless, uneven gray coat. The females give birth between February and March, depending on the geographic area. In the short time following the birth of the young, hunters move over the ice, using the most modern means available including helicopters to locate these animals. As soon as the seals are spotted, the hunters land immediately, causing the alarmed mothers to dive into the sea. The young, however, remain immobile and helpless.

Until the end of the 1960s, these hunting expeditions were carried out without any control. When several animal enthusiasts and naturalists traveled to Canada to investi-

The newborn seals have a beautiful soft white fur only during the first few months of their lives. Consequently, the young seals are extensively hunted for their valuable furs. Many people are openly concerned about the future survival of this species, as well as the cruel hunting methods used. There have been many public protests over this issue.

gate the hunting, they discovered the extremely cruel methods used to kill the seals. Often the seal cubs were only stunned before being skinned alive.

The wave of indignation and disapproval that followed the viewing of pictures and films of these slaughters (one notable film was shot by the German zoologist Bernhard Grzimek) has led to a greater control of the slaughters carried out by fur hunters. These activities have not been stopped, although Canadian authorities are quick to assure that baby seals are no longer killed by cruel methods. Animal protectionists are waging a bitter battle with the Canadian authorities over the excessive numbers of seals that are still killed. They estimate that 70 percent of the young seals are killed annually. This number is almost twice the maximum amount of hunting that could be maintained without causing a decrease in the seal population.

A large number of volunteers tries to prevent the hunters from killing the baby seals by painting their fur, which makes it useless from a commercial standpoint. However, the public authorities have been responding to this rebellious activity by imposing expensive fines, thus protecting what they consider a useful economic activity.

The world population of the harp seal is estimated at between 2.2 and 3 million animals. Of these, about 1 to 1.5 million live in the Northwest, which is practically the entire hunting zone of Canada. This latter population produces between 250,000 and 400,000 offspring per year. Of these young, 170,000 are killed annually, which represents from

A group of northern fur seals camps on a rocky coast of Alaska. This seal is the only northern species of its family. It is characterized by a thick coat of hair that has come to be known as "sealskin" in the fur trade. Because of its valuable fur, the northern fur seal has been extensively hunted in the past. Fortunately, the present hunting of this animal is strictly regulated by an international treaty which limits the numbers of animals killed annually. The objective of this policy is to maintain the population at a constant level.

40 to 70 percent of the total newborn seals. Between 1952 and the early 1970s, the commercial harvest of seals was even heavier. In that period, their population was reduced by about 50 percent. Despite the massacres, the present population remains stable. It has been learned that when the population density of the harp seal decreases, the age of sexual maturity of the females is lowered and their fertility is increased.

How much do the Canadians themselves earn from this controversial hunting of baby seals? The answer is only a few million dollars per year. In fact, the raw furs are sold to companies outside of Canada, and they make the biggest profits by treating and refining the furs. Without attempting to enter into a lengthy discussion of moral values, one might suggest that the Canadian authorities should continuously verify that the hunting of fur seals does not decrease the seal population. They should also verify that the economic return from this hunting is large enough to justify such a controversial activity.

The northern fur seal is especially vulnerable to hunting because it reproduces in very large colonies. These colonies are established by the oldest males, who are then joined by other males and females. The downward trend of the population was turned around in 1911. This resulted from an international treaty between the United States, Canada, the Soviet Union, Japan, and all other countries profiting from the harvest and sale of these furs. According to this treaty, no colony of northern fur seals can be touched. Only young males that do not live in the reproductive colonies can be hunted within established limits. A male northern fur seal must reach at least six years of age to be able to successfully face up to an encounter with the older males in the colony. The fur of these young males does not yet have scars resulting from the repeated duels between the males. Therefore, their furs are more valuable from a commercial standpoint.

THE WHITE EXPANSE OF THE GLACIERS

Water has unusual physical properties. These properties result from the asymmetric (unbalanced) structure of its molecules, with two hydrogen atoms at the base of a triangle and one oxygen atom at the vertex (top) of the triangle. The molecular structure causes the presence of voids in the ordered crystalline state. This results in a crystalline state that is less dense and "lighter" than the disordered liquid state. In other words, water reaches the temperature of maximum density above the melting point. It is for this reason that ice cubes float in a glass of water and the ice pack is found above as well as below the cold waters of the northern seas.

This difference between water and most other liquids is fundamental for life on earth. The ice floating on the polar seas forms an isolating layer over the water, which prevents it from freezing under the ice. If the sea froze at its bottom, there would be no shield against the low external temperatures. Thus the entire ocean would probably turn to ice, making life impossible over vast regions and causing unimaginable climatic upheavals.

The Ice Pack: A Dynamic Structure

The arctic ice pack varies in thickness. It ranges from a few inches on its outer margin to more than 350 feet (900 cm) in several zones. The ice pack does not have a stable form; it is subjected to seasonal as well as structural changes caused by sea currents. The rotation of the earth on its axis is a major factor in these changes.

At the beginning of winter, new ice forms on the sea's open surface. Because of the salinity of the water, it begins to freeze at a temperature of 23°F (-5°C), with the appearance of numerous small crystals that look like an oily coating. As the temperature decreases, the ice solidifies into plates that later become a continuous slab, that is, the ice pack. The ice that freezes in this simple manner never reaches a thickness of more than 6 feet (2 m). However, there are other forces that act to upset this simple landscape.

Due to the action of winds and sea currents, the ice pack breaks into large floating blocks called "floes." These floes are separated by areas of open water called "polynyas." The winds and currents cause the blocks to collide with each other. This leads to situations where one floe slides above another, forming "hummocks." These are irregular crests that sometimes reach heights of 65 to 100 feet (20 to 30 m). The hummocks give the ice pack its jagged

Opposite page: An aerial view shows the vast expanse of ice and snow in Iceland. There are permanent glaciers in the mountainous areas of this island, even though they are not far from areas that undergo a brief period of thawing.

89

The ice pack has a characteristic appearance. This is formed by large floating platforms of ice (floes) that are separated by canals of water (polynyas). The margins of these platforms have raised edges created by the force of their collisions. When the water in the canals refreezes, the ice pack becomes blocked. The ridges at the edges of the ice plates are impassible to those traveling on foot or with a snow sled.

appearance. The areas in which they occur are often impassible even with snowsleds.

In areas where the ice pack collides with other coasts, the ice may reach a height of more than 130 feet (40 m). Sometimes the accumulation of ice is so thick that the summer heat is not enough to completely melt it, and from winter to winter the ice piles up to form enormous blocks. This results in the formation of the so-called paleocrystic. These immense mountains of ice are sometimes centuries old. Huge ice blocks can break off at the coasts and drift among the thinner ice of the pack. The ice blocks stand out like white islands in a white sea, and their movements show the dynamic state of the polar ice cap. The largest of these islands of ice can be several miles wide. Their stability is such that the larger islands are sometimes used as bases for permanent scientific stations, furnished with airplane landing strips. The northern coast of Ellesmere Island is the presumed site where these colossal blocks form.

The icebergs are another source of the irregularity and the reliefs of the ice pack. Each year, the active glaciers of Greenland, Iceland, Canada, and Alaska produce about fif-

A view of the icy surface of the sea at about 81° latitude north shows several large blocks of ice. These blocks, separated from the coasts during the thaw, have become trapped, creating a group of white "islands."

teen thousand icebergs. A large part of these become incorporated into the ice pack when it forms. The largest icebergs in the Northern Hemisphere reach a length of nearly 2,000 feet (600 m) and a thickness of more than 325 feet (100 m). However, none of these can match the size of the gigantic Antarctic icebergs.

Formed by the freezing of the surface water and the addition of coastal ice, the ice pack can also increase in size from the gathering of precipitation. However, precipitation is as rare in these zones as it is in the tundra. Rain falls only in the warmest months of the year. It solidifies as small crystals of snow. Through a slow process, this snow is transformed into pack ice. The solid water passes from a complex structure with a high air content to a more compact form without air. Through this process, the density of the solid water is decreased.

On the polar ice pack, the temperatures undergo slight variations over a twenty-four-hour period. However, temperature changes through the year are much more pronounced. Near the pole, there is a difference of 104°F (40°C) between the coldest and the warmest temperatures of the

91

Several icebergs drift in the sea southeast of Alaska. Since the density of the icebergs is only slightly less than liquid water, at least five-sixths of their entire mass remains underwater. In the Northern Hemisphere, a large part of these enormous white mountains is formed by the tongues of the large Greenland glacier. They are characterized by irregular forms that differ from the shapes of the Antarctic icebergs. These latter icebergs have a tubular form because they originate from extensions of the Antarctic ice cap into the sea.

Contrary to what was previously believed, recent research has shown that the ice pack is not a rigid block but that it moves in a constant circular motion. The schematic drawing shows this circular motion (red line) according to the most recent discoveries.

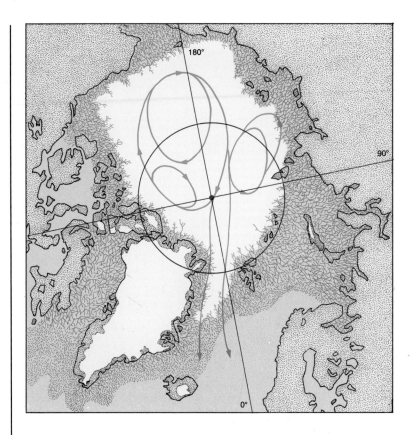

year. At latitudes above the seventieth parallel, the yearly temperature range is usually limited to between 68° and 86°F (20° and 30°C). Even in extreme cases, the highest temperatures never go above 32°F (0°C).

Usually, the short summer season is warm enough to melt the ice somewhat, opening up large areas of the sea. The meltwater has a low salt content, since part of the salt is lost at the time of freezing. Moreover, some salt is discharged into the water under the ice pack through the migrating action of the ice. This process occurs only on a small scale. It concerns the movement of dense ice masses to the bottom of the pack, and it is caused by changes in pressure and temperature.

The rare forms of life on the surface of these expanses of ice begin with the plankton. This plankton is composed of small algae and single-celled organisms called "protozoa," which develop in the meltwater pools that form over the summer. The organisms live in these pools during the brief summer when conditions are more favorable. The meltwater tends to gather in the crevasses and cracks of the

A polar bear strolls across the arctic ice. All bears have features that help them adapt more easily to colder climates. These features include a thick coat of hair, an insulating layer of fat below the skin, large body size, and the capacity to hibernate during the coldest months of the year. The polar bear is not greatly different from the bears of the temperate and tropical regions. However, its diet has become more carnivorous, making it the largest land predator in the world.

ice. It can flow through the fractures of the pack and reach the cold layers of ice below, where it freezes again. It may even come into contact with the layer of saline water that holds the ice pack afloat. The temperature of this water is normally near the freezing point, and it is lower than the temperature of the water coming from the surface. When the two waters come in contact, a soft ice is formed that contains large bubbles of sea water. The bubble will freeze during the following winter.

The King of the Ice

The arctic ice pack has often been compared to a desert. This comparison may be totally valid, depending on how one interprets the word *desert*. It is true that the expanse of ice, like the expanses of sand and rock in the tropics, is a particularly difficult environment. Like the Sahara and many other large deserts, the ice pack has its share of life forms. It is inhabited by various species of seals, whales, dolphins, arctic fox, seabirds, fish, shellfish, and many other marine organisms that thrive in its waters. The polar bear, however, is the animal that truly dominates this region. It is the largest of all the land carnivores in the world.

Relatively speaking, this great carnivore belongs to a

The paw of the polar bear is compared with that of the brown bear. The polar bear paw has a greater covering of hair, which prevents heat loss from its extremities. This extra hair also enables the polar bear to walk over ice and snow without slipping.

fairly new species. It would appear that this species evolved at the beginning of the last glaciation, about a hundred thousand years ago. The polar bear developed from a northern bear (perhaps Siberian). Its fur became white, thick, and impenetrable, and its body underwent a series of changes that adapted the animal to a life in the extreme North. For example, the hair of the coat is long and erect. Because the hairs are hollow, they have great insulating capacity. The hairs are also transparent, allowing the sun to reach the black skin, which is adapted to absorbing as much heat as possible from the sun's rays.

A thick layer of fat under the skin maintains the bear's body temperature at a high level. This fat stores precious amounts of food energy. The fat layer is so effective that this giant is forced to cool itself by entering the water of the arctic seas.

The only other significant difference between the polar bear and its relative, the brown bear, is the structure of the paws. The polar bear's paws have remained wide and flat, while the claws are shorter, thicker, and very sharp. A membrane grows between the toes, uniting them for over half of their length. Thus the paws have an extended surface support that is covered with fur on the bottom. The features of the paws enable the polar bear to easily move over both fresh snow and the smoothest and most compact ice. On the ice pack, the polar bear reaches a speed of 19 miles (30 km) per hour. It manages to climb up even the steepest crests and can move as silently as a cat.

The two necessary elements of the polar bear's normal hunting technique are its camouflage and the extreme caution of its movements. Once it has spotted a resting seal, the polar bear carefully approaches, making sure to cut off any escape routes that the seal could take. Before attacking the seal, the polar bear moves to a surprisingly close distance.

The polar bear's various hunting tricks have been extensively described by naturalists who have studied the animal. During its long wanderings over the ice pack, this bear is able to locate dens of ringed seals buried more than 3 feet (1 m) beneath the snow, due to its highly-developed sense of smell. It can patiently wait for hours for a seal to exit from its breathing hole, at which point it captures it with a lightning-fast swipe of its paw. The polar bear has also been known to swim underwater beneath the seal's breathing holes, jumping out to surpise its prey. The polar bear is a very efficient killer. It can immobilize its prey with one blow

polar bear

brown bear

96

The polar bear uses several techniques to hunt seals, which are its primary source of food. The bear surprises a resting seal after swimming under the water, cutting off all possible escape routes *(top)*. Covering its black nose with a paw in order to better camouflage itself, the giant predator can wait for hours outside the breathing hole of a seal, ready to capture its prey with one swipe of its paw *(bottom left)*. Thanks to its keen sense of smell, the polar bear is able to locate seal cubs left by the mother in dens excavated in the ice *(bottom right)*. It reaches them by digging with its powerful paws.

of the claws and quickly kill it off with a bite at the neck, breaking the spinal cord.

Because of its perfected hunting techniques, the polar bear even preys on musk oxen and small walruses, which are usually well protected by the adults. It has even been known to attack humans, according to several accounts of scientific expeditions in the Arctic Circle. But whenever possible, the bears feed on the meat of whales.

In the summer, when plates of ice of various sizes begin to separate from the coast, the bears move toward the interior and change their diets. In this period, they feed primarily on roots, leaves, fruits, small rodents, and the eggs and chicks of ground-nesting birds.

The biology of the polar bear is well known, thanks to a significant international program of research begun in the early 1970s. This program resulted from the concerns expressed by zoologists at a seminar in Fairbanks, Alaska, in 1965. At that time, more than 2,000 polar bears were killed —every year hunters killed between 1,200 and 1,400 in

Canada, and more than 1,000 in the remaining arctic areas. Up until that time, little was known of the population of this species, its movements, reproduction, or life span. No one was able to determine the number of polar bears that could be killed without reducing the population. In the meantime, the polar bears were even being shot from the decks of icebreaker ships and tourist planes. This uncontrolled massacre threatened to spell the end of one of the most extraordinary carnivores of the planet.

To avoid that, the International Union for the Conservation of Nature established the Specialist Group for the Polar Bear in 1968. The group included scientists from Denmark (Greenland), Norway (Svalbard Islands), the Soviet Union (the northern coasts and Wrangel Island), the United States (Alaska), and Canada (the Northwest Territories and Hudson Bay), territories lying within the polar regions inhabited by the polar bear.

Conservation efforts had already begun in Russia in 1956. A government decree, in fact, protected the bear cubs all year around. Despite this law, however, the population of Russian bears showed a dramatic drop. This was primarily caused by the bears' migrations to Alaska and the Svalbard Islands, where they were still widely hunted. From 1966 to 1969, over one hundred bears were marked in the Svalbard Islands as part of an experiment. By 1970, thirty-nine of these had already been killed by hunters.

In 1973, after a series of partial hunting restrictions, it was decided to completely abolish the hunting of polar bears throughout all of the Arctic Basin. The traditional hunters of this animal, the Eskimos, were excepted from this agreement. Research conducted on the different bear populations soon revealed the ban's positive effects. The trend of a declining population was turned around, and within a short period of time, the distribution of the species had returned to its original levels.

Various marking techniques, such as radio collars, have facilitated the study of the polar bear's behavior. These studies have revealed unexpected aspects of the life of the "king of the ice." For example, it was discovered that polar bears are extremely individualistic animals. They do not have a defined territory, but roam over the ice pack endlessly searching for food. There are no fixed ties between the males and the females. They live together only during the brief mating period, from April to May.

At certain times of the year, their movements cease to

Opposite page: A group of polar bears gathers at Cape Churchill, Canada. Normally polar bears are not social animals, but occasionally one can find a small group consisting of a mother and its young of up to two years of age. Sometimes groups of bears can be seen in areas where there is an abundance of food.

A female polar bear, walking over the ice, is followed by two cubs. The young of this species live with the mother for almost two years. During this period, they learn all the difficult techniques of hunting and survival. This enables them to inhabit an environment that at first glance appears to be absolutely unsuitable for any type of animal life other than fish, birds, or sea mammals.

be casual, and the bears begin to move in a precise direction. When the temperature rises, they can be found on the floating ice sheets that drift in the polar regions. In the summer, they move southward toward the margin of the ice pack and then toward the border between the tundra and the forests. Here they feed on berries, the only fruit they like to eat. Normally only the males and the youngest females migrate. The mature females, which are those over four years of age, tend to gather on the small hilly islands beyond the Arctic Circle. It is here that they dig deep dens in the snow that are used to give birth to their cubs. The impor-

tance of these islands, such as Wrangel and the Svalbards, is considerable. In an area of less than 3/10 of a sq. mile (1 sq. km), one may find up to fifty birthing dens.

A pregnant female sometimes sets out on extremely long journeys to reach the site where she gives birth. She may cover a daily distance of 25 miles (40 km) on foot and by swimming. The total distance may be hundreds of miles. Many bears travel to the Norwegian polar islands from Greenland, while the Alaskan bears travel to the Soviet Arctic north of eastern Siberia.

The embryo remains dormant until September, when the short pregnancy actually begins. One to three cubs are born at the end of January. By this time, the female has already been in the den for two months, sheltered from the extreme temperatures of the outside. The body heat of the bear maintains the temperature inside the ice den near 32°F (0°C). This temperature is adequate for the newborn cubs.

The cubs barely weigh 1 pound (.5 kg) at birth. They are blind and furless and measure about 12 inches (30 cm). The mother bear does not eat anything for several months. Nursing on the mother's milk, the cubs already weigh close to 45 pounds (20 kg) by the time they first poke their noses out of the den. The den is opened around the first days of March, but it is not abandoned for another week.

The bond between the mother and the cubs is strong. Throughout the first year of their lives, the cubs live with the mother. They also spend the next winter together in a common den. During these winter months, while nursing the cubs, the female bear fasts again, surviving by drawing on the fat reserves under its skin. By the second spring, the young bears have already reached the size of a large dog. They now finally begin to take an active part in hunting. They learn to hunt by following the mother and imitating her movements. At this point they are sufficiently independent to withstand the long migrations over the ice and through the water.

The population of the polar bear doubled in the first ten years after becoming a protected species. The present population has been estimated at about twenty thousand animals. However, many dangers still menace this and other arctic species. The delicate ecological balance of the polar regions is also threatened by pollution and the disturbance caused by the mining of mineral resources. The impact of these factors could eventually have a much deadlier effect than hunting.

GUIDE TO AREAS OF NATURAL INTEREST

Up to a certain point, the great North can be toured with a normal motor vehicle or with simple mountain-climbing equipment for excursions in the mountains. In Norway, Sweden, Finland, Canada, and Alaska, the roads are in excellent condition, and there are towns and centers with basic tourist facilities and accommodations. In these regions of the North, the various areas of natural interest are not only vast, spectacular, and interesting, but they are generally well organized for visitors. They have guided trails, shelters, visitor centers, and printed information.

However, it is necessary to keep in mind that the farther north one travels, the fewer settlements he or she will find. The population density drops to extremely low levels. For example, in the entire country of Canada, there are an average of 5.5 inhabitants per square mile (2.2 per sq. km), while in the Northwest Territories there are .02 inhabitants per square mile (.01 per sq. km). The Eskimos living beyond the northern limit of the forests, from eastern Asia to Greenland, do not number more than fifty thousand.

It is advisable to plan a trip in these areas very carefully, always keeping an adequate supply of gasoline and essential spare parts on hand. It is a good idea to buy an insurance policy from a reputable company that will pay for emergency rescues should need arise.

Obviously, summer is the only season in which a trip to these areas is practical, particularly during the months of June and July. Generally, overcast skies should be expected. Therefore, one must be quick to take advantage of the favorable photographic opportunities. One consolation is that the days are very long. If one is able to get by with little sleep, there is much time available for visiting the natural areas.

Certain faraway regions can be reached only by means of helicopters, private airplanes, or sleds drawn by dogs. Excursions into these areas should always be led by expert guides. If one intends to travel far beyond the Arctic Circle, he or she will be faced with serious bureaucratic as well as security problems. On Hudson Bay and the Svalbard Islands, during the summer for example, there is a serious danger of being killed by polar bears. In some areas of the tundra, traveling on foot is prohibited. In any case, when attempting these trips, one should have a thorough knowledge of the areas, find a sponsor to cover the considerable expenses incurred, and never forget that inexperience and carelessness can result in tragedy.

Opposite page: The coastal region near Heimaey, Iceland, offers a panoramic view. The wooden structures in the photograph are used by the local people for drying fish. Living in the rigorous lands of the North requires particular adaptations on the part of both animals and humans. A person visiting these areas for any length of time should conform to the customs and precautions of the local people. These local customs have enabled them to live in these regions for many centuries.

The map indicates the main areas of natural interest in the arctic regions of Eurasia and North America.

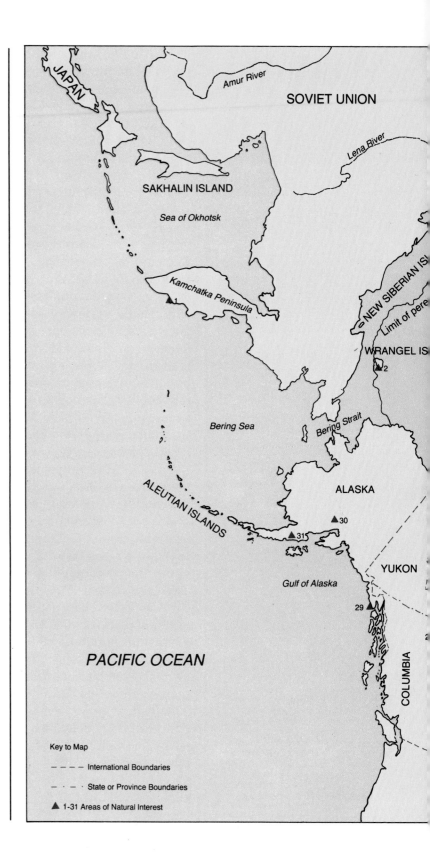

Key to Map

- – – – International Boundaries

– · – · State or Province Boundaries

▲ 1-31 Areas of Natural Interest

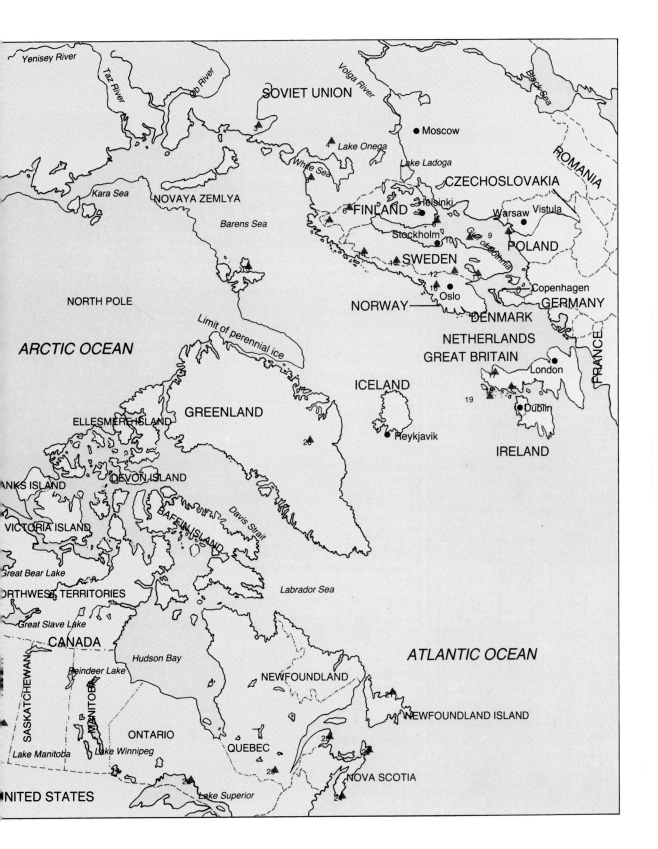

ARCTIC OCEAN

NORTH POLE

Yenisey River

Taz River

Ob River

Kara Sea

NOVAYA ZEMLYA

Barens Sea

SOVIET UNION

Volga River

Black Sea

● Moscow

Lake Onega

Lake Ladoga

ROMANIA

White Sea

CZECHOSLOVAKIA

FINLAND

Helsinki

Warsaw Vistula

●

Stockholm

Gulf of Bothnia

POLAND

●

SWEDEN

Copenhagen

GERMANY

Oslo

●

NORWAY

DENMARK

Limit of perennial ice

NETHERLANDS

GREAT BRITAIN

London

●

ICELAND

19

Reykjavik

●

Dublin

●

GREENLAND

IRELAND

ELLESMERE ISLAND

DEVON ISLAND

20

BANKS ISLAND

Davis Strait

BAFFIN ISLAND

VICTORIA ISLAND

Great Bear Lake

Labrador Sea

NORTHWEST TERRITORIES

Great Slave Lake

CANADA

Hudson Bay

ATLANTIC OCEAN

Reindeer Lake

NEWFOUNDLAND

SASKATCHEWAN

MANITOBA

ONTARIO

Lake Winnipeg

NEWFOUNDLAND ISLAND

Lake Manitoba

QUEBEC

NOVA SCOTIA

UNITED STATES

Lake Superior

SOVIET UNION

Kronotski (1)

This reserve of 3,720 sq. miles (9,640 sq. km) occupies part of the eastern coast of the Kamchatka Peninsula on the Pacific Ocean. The peninsula has a considerable amount of volcanic activity, similar to Alaska, which is located just opposite to it on the other side of the sea. Geysers, hot springs, and volcanoes are found in this reserve. The vegetation is typical of the tundra, although its composition changes according to the altitude. The most characteristic plants are several species of birch and dropworts that are restricted to an area within Soviet Asia. Several interesting mammals are the Kamchatka marmot, the arctic ground squirrel, the brown bear, and the reindeer. Salmon are found in the rivers, and ringed seals and Steller sea lions are common in the coastal waters.

Several parts of the reserve can be visited with excursions organized and conducted by local personnel. The nearest large city is Petropavlosk.

Wrangel (2)

This island in the Chukchi Sea is uniformly covered by tundra vegetation. It has been subjected to the restrictions of a natural reserve due to its importance in the biology of the polar bear. Bears migrate here from a vast region facing the northern coasts of the Soviet Union. From 100 to 250 pregnant female polar bears arrive on the island in September and October. They then take shelter in dens dug under the ice and snow, where they wait to give birth to the cubs.

The vegetation of the island is composed of dwarf birches, arctic willows, sedges, and reindeer "moss," which is actually a lichen. This lichen is the basic food for a total population of about five thousand reindeer. Occasionally, thousands of walruses will gather along the coasts.

All 2,700 sq. miles (7,000 sq. km) of the island are protected. Access is permitted only to scientists studying the polar bear or the snow goose.

Pechora (3)

The Pechora River flows from the Ural Mountains in a northerly direction, crossing a vast region of tundra before flowing into the Barents Sea. Throughout its 1,120-mile (nearly 1,800 km) course, it goes through areas of the taiga and tundra, before emptying into the Arctic Ocean. Its waters abound with such cold-water game fish as salmon and whitefish.

Part of the Pechora River is included in the Pechora-Ilychsky Reserve, where the Ilychsky and the Pechora rivers meet. This is a hilly region where traces of Paleolithic hunting settlements and other fossil remains can still be seen.

Because of the latitude, the vegetation of this area is typical of the taiga, with a predominance of Scotch pine and larch trees, depending on the elevation. There are forty-three species of mammals here, including beavers, wolverines, sable, moose, wolves, and bears. Reindeer range over an area extending from the treeless northern lowlands to this reserve. Among the birds of this area are ptarmigans, perching birds, and woodpeckers of the taiga.

The reserve can be visited if accompanied by a tour guide or with the permission of the administration. The protected area is 186 miles (300 km) from the city of Pechora.

Darvinsky (4)

This reserve, located about 210 miles (350 km) north of Moscow, occupies a large part of the southern region of the taiga. This territory encloses many wetlands covered with vast carpets of sphagnum moss, while the marginal land is covered by lichens. About forty species of mammals are found here, including lynx and moose. The more than two hundred species of birds include geese, ducks, ospreys, sea eagles, ptarmigans, and mountain francolins. The common European viper also inhabits the reserve.

Studies on ptarmigans and marsh ecosystems are conducted in this protected area. The reserve is totally protected, and visitors are not permitted. However, it is possible to visit the surrounding areas.

Soviet Lapland and the White Sea (5)

The Lapp territory of the Kola Peninsula juts out into the Barents Sea eastward from the border with Finland. The terrain of this region is similar to the lake country within Finland, and a large part of it is well protected. The western extremity of the Kandalaksha Bay is a reserve of 135 sq. miles (350 sq. km), while the region south of Murmansk belongs to the Laplandsky reserve. Both reserves have a typical taiga vegetation, dominated by Scotch pine and Norway spruce trees. The animal species inhabiting the park are characteristic of the northern Asian and northeastern European regions. These include the Siberian titmouse, the Siberian jay, and all the European species of grouse and ptarmigans, as well as the mountain francolin. Further inland, the vegetation of the tundra is characterized by lichens, scattered arctic willow, Lapp rhododendron, and white mountain avens.

A log cabin sits alone on the snowy landscape of the Central Siberian taiga. Many destinations in the great North are not easily reached because of the long distances, climatic difficulties, and the scarcity or lack of overnight lodgings and services. However, the Soviet taiga has an excellent system of air and rail transportation as well as numerous tourist facilities.

Several types of mammals live in the reserve, such as beavers, lemmings, brown bears, martens, wolverines, otters, moose, and more than twenty thousand reindeer, which migrate between the forests and the open zones. Gyrfalcons, golden eagles, and ospreys can be seen flying in the sky.

The islands are covered with tundra and are occupied by colonies of seabirds that include eider ducks, jaegers, skuas, great black-backed gulls, herring gulls, three-toed gulls, dovekies, Brünnich's murres, common murres, and Atlantic puffins.

Both reserves are headquarters for scientific research. Presently no visitors are allowed to enter the reserve.

FINLAND

Oulanka (6)

This national park covers an area of about 39 sq. miles (100 sq. km) in northeastern Finland, near the border with the Soviet Union. The park includes vast conifer forests, fifty lakes, and beautiful rivers with rapids and waterfalls. Among the animals that live in the park are reindeer, moose, martens, varying hares, and many birds, such as Siberian jays, the rare bluetail, and the large-headed owlet.

Pallas-Ounastunturi (7)

This national park extends over an area of 193 sq. miles (500 sq. km) and is located on a plateau of the Lapland mountain chain. The park includes a vast area of tundra north of the conifer forest. The landscape is formed by a typical mixture of trees and open peat bogs, inhabited by animals typical of the northern ecosystems.

Aland (8)

The 6,544 islands of the Aland archipelago are located in the Baltic Sea across from the Finnish mainland. These islands are presently rising out of the water at the rate of about 13/32 of an inch (1 cm) per year.

The vegetation includes both pastures and mixed forests of broad-leaved trees and conifers. Many species of animals live in the islands, such as moose, deer, ermine, otters, seals, grouse, greylag geese, sea eagles, and swans.

POLAND

Vistola (9)

This reserve is located between the mouth of the Vistula River and its slow-moving western branch. It is one of the most important areas of continental Europe for the study of migratory shorebirds.

The most numerous visitor is the black-bellied sandpiper, but other rarer species are also present. The long coastline is characterized by numerous marshes and two large lagoons. These are ideal environments for numerous species of ducks, such as pintails, gadwalls, great scaups, mergansers, and grebes. The vegetation is composed of a continuous forest of Scotch pines, part of which lies in the protected reserve of Ptiza Rhay ("bird paradise").

SWEDEN

Bla Jungfrin (10)

This national park is found in a small, red-granite island in the Baltic Sea. It has a forest of Scotch pine, oaks, and other broad-leafed trees. The most significant animal here is the sea eagle, but there are also black guillemots and eider ducks. The park is reached by boat from the north-western part of Öland. Overnight stays are not possible.

Stora Mosse-Kävsjon (11)

This nature reserve of 25 sq. miles (65 sq. km) is one of the largest protected areas south of Lapland. Hunting, fishing, and public access are strictly regulated. It includes a vast marsh with reliefs (raised surfaces, elevations) alternating with open water. A large number of aquatic birds nests in the marsh, including loons, swans, widegears, and snipes. During the migratory periods, there are a large number of geese. Bird-watching is facilitated by a number of walkways and an observation tower.

The Scotch pine is the predominant tree of the forest. The three-toed woodpecker lives in this tree along with many perching birds. This environment is ideal for the growth of many types of orchids.

Sarek (12)

This national park is located along the border with Norway. It includes about 7 sq. miles (19 sq. km) of the Scandinavian mountain chain. A tundra vegetation typical of high elevations grows near the approximately one hundred glaciers. Common plants are the white mountain avens and the northern monk's hood. The most notable animals are the golden eagle, the violet sandpiper, and the gyrfalcon. The delta of the Rapa River, which flows into Lake Laidaure, is interesting and rich with birds.

Hunting and fishing are prohibited for everyone except Lapps, who derive most of their food from these activities. Overnight stays are permitted only to university researchers.

Padjelanta (13)

This park of 772 sq. miles (2,000 sq. km) is located in Swedish Lapland in an area of plateaus, glacial lakes, and moist alpine meadows. The meadow vegetation is of the arctic type. Different species of willows grow in the lowest areas, while dwarf birch trees grow in areas with elevations a little higher. The predominant plant in areas of high elevation is the mossplant, which is a low, heathlike evergreen shrub.

The animal species include Norway lemmings, arctic fox, red fox, brown bear, wolverine, lynx, and moose. Some of the birds are loons, geese, rough-legged buzzards, rock ptarmigans, and long-tailed jaegers. Occasionally, wolves and gyrfalcons are found in the park. Only Lapps are allowed to hunt and fish in the park.

Lodgings can be found in the park, and camping is also permitted. The park is visited by about five thousand persons each year.

Paljekajse (14)

This national park is located at the same latitude as the Arctic Circle, at the southern boundaries of Lapland. Its 56 sq. miles (146 sq. km) cover a mountainous area of birch forests, lakes, marshes, and alpine moors. Various species of alpine and northern birch trees dominate two-thirds of the territory. The forests offer refuge for mammals typical of the marginal forested areas. These animals include varying hares, red fox, ermine, wolverine, and moose. Only Lapps are permitted to hunt these animals.

The park has several hiking trails. There are Lapp shelters along the trails where hikers can spend the night.

NORWAY

Svalbard (15)

The largest and most interesting protected areas in Norway are found on the Svalbard Islands. Three national parks and one nature reserve cover about half their territory. Primarily, arctic animal species live in these areas. The most important reserve is the Northeastern Svalbard Reserve, which covers an area of 6,000 sq. miles (15,550 sq. km). The three national parks are Southeast Svalbard, South Spitzbergen, and Northwest Spitzbergen. The vegetation is typical of the high tundra, especially in the northern islands, which are 80 percent covered with ice. On the island of Nordanstlandet, as many as eighty-three species of seed-bearing plants and ferns have been identified. These plants represent about half of all the plant species on the island.

The most significant mammals are polar bears, arctic fox, ringed seals, bearded seals, and walruses, which are very rare in the European seas. The musk ox was reintroduced to the islands in 1929.

There are seventeen species of birds that regularly nest on these islands. The most numerous are the murres. The ivory gulls and Sabine gulls are more interesting than the murres. The only area in Europe where they nest is the islands of Franz Josef. There are also fulmars, sandpipers, ptarmigans, snow buntings, red phalaropes, and arctic terns.

Rondane (16)

The Rondane National Park extends over an area of 231 sq. miles (600 sq. km). Its elevation varies from 3,280 to 6,560 feet (1,000 to 2,000 m). A splendid tundra covers the park, along with a few scattered birch woods. The zone has a wide variety of animal life. There are moose, reindeer, roe deer, musk oxen (introduced), lynx, wolverine, and 124 species of birds.

The road that runs north from Oslo, near Lillehammer, leads to this park. Hiking is the only permissible means of touring the protected territory.

GREAT BRITAIN

Rannoch Moor (17)

This nature reserve of 6 sq. miles (15 sq. km) is managed by the Nature Conservancy Council and is located in central Scotland, about 60 miles (100 km) northwest of Edinburgh. The reserve is not frequently visited by tourists. Evident traces of the glacial activity of the Pleistocene epoch are found throughout the area. Examples are ridges of glacial deposits and granite located among lakes of all sizes. On the hillsides exposed to the sun, heaths and heathers represent the dominant vegetation. A local population of about two hundred deer inhabits this area. Carpets of sphagnum moss grow in wet depressions in the ground.

The birds that nest here include ptarmigans, golden plovers, greenshanks, black-bellied sandpipers, and marsh owls.

Cairngorms (18)

This nature reserve extends over an area of 96 sq. miles (250 sq. km) in the Scottish Highlands. The reserve is interesting for the significant traces left by the activity of the past glaciers and the presence of a reindeer herd, which was introduced in the area in the 1950s. The reindeer thrive in this environment, which is very similar to their original habitats.

The reserve can be reached from Aviemore, or Kingcraig, located just a few miles from the boundaries of the protected zone. At Loch Garten (close to Aviemore), there is a well-known nesting site of the osprey. This site is

Autumn comes to a forest in Alaska. Whoever undertakes a trip in the far North—even in the areas that are considered most accessible, like Alaska —must keep in mind that many areas are sparsely populated and have vast dimensions.

equipped with cabins and trails for visitors.

This island of 40 sq. miles (105 sq. km) is a totally protected nature reserve. This is the area of Scotland where the sea eagle was reintroduced. The spreading of this bird has been facilitated by the uneven terrain of the island, with rocky peaks and heath moors. Deer are common, and there are numerous seabirds. Access to the park is not easy, and lodgings are limited. Boat service between the island and the mainland is offered four days a week.

Rum (19)

DENMARK

Greenland (20)

Denmark's most important park is the Greenland National Park, which is under the jurisdiction of Denmark. The park covers a territory of 270,200 sq. miles (700,000 sq. km), and it is administered by a special government official. Plants and animals are typically arctic. The largest glaciers of the Northern Hemisphere are united in one mass in the Greenland ice cap. The land and the surrounding seas are covered with ice for eight months of the year. The vegetation is relatively rich in several zones, and it is composed of arctic willows, dwarf birch, mountain grasses, tundra grasses, and various small heathberry and blueberry shrubs.

The typical northern animals that can be observed here are arctic hares, collared lemmings, arctic fox, several hundred polar bears, ermine, musk oxen, gyrfalcons, and ptarmigans. Marsh owls, brants, barnacle geese, old-squaw ducks, three-toed sandpipers, and greater sandpipers are the most characteristic birds of this area. Very large colonies of seabirds are found on the islands and the coasts, which have many fiords. These seabirds include Iceland gulls, glaucous gulls, black guillemots, and dovekies. The areas are also inhabited by various species of seals, such as ringed seals, harp seals, walruses, bearded seals, and hooded seals. Belugas and narwhales swim in the open waters nearby.

Human settlements are scarce, but there is an airport at Mestersvig. There are presently no tourist activities, but visits to the points of greatest natural and archeological interest will soon be permitted. There are archeological finds here that date back to 3000 B.C.

CANADA

Newfoundland:
Terra Nova (21)

Unlike the other Canadian parks mentioned below, the Terra Nova National Park is found in an area with jagged terrain, numerous bays, and long, deep fiords inserted into the offshoots of the Appalachian Mountain chain. Due to the effect of the cold ocean currents, the vegetation is typical of the northern forests, interspersed with marshy areas of sphagnum moss and shrubs associated with wetland zones.

The most remarkable animal is the moose, accompanied by numerous other mammals and birds. The osprey and the bald eagle nest here. Blackfish dolphins and several species of seals can be observed in their habitats in the sea.

Nova Scotia: Cape Breton Highlands (22)

This national park of 366 sq. miles (950 sq. km) is located at the northern tip of Nova Scotia, on a triangle of land bounded on two sides by the ocean and on one side by the interior plateau of the peninsula. The long sandy and pebbly beaches are inhabited by numerous aquatic birds as well as by bald eagles. The ruffed grouse and the recently introduced caribou live in the mixed forests of this national park.

There are many wetlands within the park, including many small lakes and vast areas of muskeg. These areas are inhabited by muskrats, otters, and beavers. The highest slopes are dry and covered with lichens.

Campsites and cabins are available, and they can be reached by the highway.

Nova Scotia: Kejimkujik (23)

This national park of 143 sq. miles (370 sq. km) is located in the interior of southern Nova Scotia. It offers a variety of evidence of past glacial action. There are eskers, rounded and irregular rock masses, and rock beds that have been grooved and smoothed by the passage of the glaciers. Among the lower reliefs of the plateau, there are many deep lakes, surrounded by mixed forests that are inhabited by numerous animals. The park is reached by the highway, and there are campsites available.

Quebec: Forillon (24)

The regions surrounding the Gulf of St. Lawrence include a considerable number of national parks of a relatively limited size. Some of these parks are important for the animals they host or for their landforms. The Forillon National Park is located at the tip of the Gaspe Peninsula. The most interesting features are the birds, including gannets, herring gulls, three-toed gulls, black guillemots, and other seabirds. Camping is not permitted within the park, but both rustic and civilized accommodations can be found on the outskirts of the park.

This park encloses another hilly region, characterized by the presence of numerous valleys excavated by the glaciers. The dominant vegetation is a forest with a large variety of conifer trees, which are inhabited by numerous small perching birds. The trees include several different species of pine, spruce, fir, and cedar. Several types of characteristic mammals of the taiga are present in the park, with the exception of the caribou.

Of all the Canadian parks, this is perhaps the most accessible park for the nature-loving tourist. It also has some of the best facilities for visitors.

This national park covers an area of 725 sq. miles (1,878 sq. km). It is located in a region characterized by numerous lakes surrounded by forests of fir and birch trees. Its relatively southern location results in a mild climate despite the proximity to the open expanses of the tundra. The park includes 50 miles (80 km) of shoreline along Lake Superior. Besides the usual mammals, there are also beavers, muskrats, and minks. The birds here include ruffed grouse and many shorebirds, such as snipes and sandpipers.

This hilly region has particularly interesting rock formations. It is a plateau formed by the action of glaciers, which left behind many accumulations of glacial deposits. The area is also dotted by small lakes and marshes. Wolves, brown bears, lynx, moose, and caribou are some of the larger mammals found in this park. The abundance of water attracts the nesting bald eagles. An area of about 4 sq. miles (10 sq. km) of the Waskwei River, as well as an area of 65 sq. miles (168 sq. km) of the Wildcat Hill Reserve are protected. Fossil-bearing clay layers and large areas of muskeg are found along the river that drains the entire plateau. Organized camping areas are available outside the park boundaries.

A series of parks arranged like a semicircle around Hudson Bay is found south of the sixtieth parallel. They face the northern band of the forest. The most important of these is the Wood Buffalo National Park which covers an area of 17,295 sq. miles (44,807 sq. km). As suggested by the name of the park, the most significant inhabitant is the wood buffalo. There are also black bear, moose, caribou, about forty other species of mammals, and two hundred species of birds—the widest variety of taiga animals in all of North America. The vastness of the territory and the variety of habitats attract numerous species of animals.

There are sixteen campsites in the park, as well as lodgings in the nearby cities of Hay River and Fort Smith. More than one hundred thousand people visit the park every year.

UNITED STATES

Alaska:
Glacier Bay (29)

Alaska contains some of the largest protected areas of the United States, as well as some of the most spectacular areas of the entire North American arctic zone. The most important of these is Glacier Bay, with an area of 5,056 sq. miles (13,100 sq. km). This is a region with a series of ridges that rapidly slopes from sea level to elevations of more than 14,760 feet (4,500 m). Many glaciers are found between its peaks, twenty of which have tongues reaching all the way to the sea. Many glacier beds have become fiords and are filled by sea water.

During the last 150 years, a large part of this territory has been covered by a taiga vegetation of pines, spruces, firs, and hemlocks. On the margins of the taiga, one can still observe the various stages of plant successions. The low elevation forests are interspersed with muskeg, and they are inhabited by many mammals. These include brown and black bears, wolverines, wolves, otters, lynx, moose, and mule deer. On the coast there are numerous seabirds and marine mammals, including the rare humpback and finback whales.

The glaciers and fiords are important tourist attractions. The park can be reached by plane or by boat, and it offers limited lodging possibilities.

Alaska:
Mount McKinley (30)

The name of this park is taken from the name of the highest peak in North America, which reaches an elevation of 20,321 feet (6,194 m). The park occupies an area of 3,018 sq. miles (7,820 sq. km). It is covered by forests only at elevations below 2,624 feet (800 m). These forests consist of fir, spruce, birch, American larch, and poplar. There are areas of wet tundra (muskeg) as well as alpine tundra beyond the treeline. Thirty–seven species of mammals are present in the park. There are many fowl-like birds, including three species of ptarmigans and two types of ruffed grouse. Other birds that nest here are the arctic tern, the golden plover, the long-tailed jaeger, and the wheatear.

The park has ample tourist facilities. Its campsites host more than one hundred thousand visitors every year.

Following pages: Sleds are pulled by dogs during an expedition to the North Pole. The dog sled is the only available means of transportation over the ice pack.

The Katmai National Monument is located at the base of the Alaska Peninsula, and it rivals Glacier Bay in size and attractions. It covers an area of 4,902 sq. miles (12,700 sq. km) with a variety of characteristic northern environments. This park includes 99 miles (160 km) of coastline with numerous bays, fiords, and lagoons. Further inland, the landscape changes to northern forest and wet tundra. This type of vegetation follows the Aleutian Highlands up to an elevation of from 2,000 to 2,300 feet (600 to 700 m), where it is replaced by a dry alpine tundra. Blue spruce and paper birch characterize the large band of forest. At the edges of this forest, near the sea and further inland, one finds alders, willows, and a type of birch. Heaths, bearberries, and mountain avens grow in the areas of higher elevation, above which only bare land and numerous volcanic peaks are found. The highest peak reaches an elevation of 7,585 feet (2,312 m).

The park contains the unique Valley of the Ten Thousand Smokes. This was formed in 1912 by the eruption that destroyed Mount Katmai. Several hundred smoke holes that were opened at that time are still active today.

The animal population is equally notable. On the coasts there are numerous sea mammals, such as the beluga, the gray whale, the sea otter, the harbor seal, the Steller sea lion, and the northern fur seal. Animals living inland include brown bears, wolves, foxes, wolverines, lynx, moose, and caribou. Numerous bald eagles nest here.

There are four camping areas equipped with cabins and tents, available for visitors.

GLOSSARY

adaptation change or adjustment by which a species or individual improves its condition in relationship to its environment.

algae primitive organisms which resemble plants but do not have true roots, stems, or leaves. Algae are usually found in water or damp places.

archipelago a group or chain of many islands.

aurora borealis shining bands or streamers of light sometimes appearing in the night sky of the Northern Hemisphere, believed to be electrical charges in the air.

biogeography the branch of biology that deals with the geographical distribution of plants and animals.

carnivore a meat-eating organism such as a predatory mammal, bird of prey, or insectivorous plant.

conifers cone-bearing trees and shrubs, most of which are evergreens.

conservation the controlled use and systematic protection of natural resources, such as forests and waterways.

cyclone a windstorm with a violent, whirling movement. Cyclones are centers of low pressure which move over the continents, carrying bad weather and destructive forces.

dominant the species of plant or animal which is most numerous in a community, and which has control over the other organisms in its environment. Dominant species always grow in great numbers.

ecology the relationship between organisms and their environment. The science and study of ecology is extremely important as a means of preserving all the forms of life on earth.

environment the circumstances or conditions of a plant or animal's surroundings. The physical and social conditions of an organism's environment influence its growth and development.

erosion natural processes such as weathering, abrasion, and corrosion, by which material is removed from the earth's surface.

esker a winding, narrow ridge of sand or gravel, probably deposited by a stream flowing in or under glacial ice.

evolution a gradual process in which something changes into a different and usually more complex or better form.

extinction the process of destroying or extinguishing. Many species of plant and animal life face extinction either because of natural changes in the environment or those caused by the carelessness of humans.

fiord a narrow inlet or arm of the sea bordered by steep cliffs.

fossil a remnant or trace of an organism of a past geological age, such as a skeleton or leaf imprint, embedded in some part of the earth's crust.

habitat the area or type of environment in which a person or other organism normally occurs. Specific environmental factors are necessary for providing a "natural" habitat for all living things.

humid containing a large amount of water or water vapor. Warm air currents help to produce a humid environment.

lichen a primitive plant formed by the association of blue-green algae with fungi. Lichens form part of the tundra environment of the far north.

loess a fine-grained, yellowish brown, extremely fertile soil.

mammoth any of a group of extinct elephants having hairy skin and long tusks curving upward. Mammoth remains have been found in glacial deposits in North America.

monogamy the practice of having only one mate.

moraine a mass of rocks, gravel, sand, and clay carried and deposited by a glacier. Moraines are simply layers or ridges of rubble which form at the sides or ends of a glacier.

muskeg a kind of bog or marsh containing thick layers of decaying vegetable matter, mosses, etc., found especially in Canada and Alaska.

paleontology the branch of geology that deals with prehistoric forms of life through the study of plant and animal fossils.

parasite an organism that grows, feeds, and is sheltered on or in a different organism while contributing nothing to the survival of its host.

pemmican dried, lean meat pounded into a paste with fat, and preserved in the form of pressed cakes. The American Indians prepared and ate pemmican until very recent times.

physiology the branch of biology dealing with the function and processes of living organisms or their parts and organs.

plankton microscopic plant and animal organisms which float or drift in the ocean or in bodies of fresh water. Plankton represents an important food source for many animals.

polynya an oblong area of open water surrounded by sea ice, or floes.

precipitation water droplets or ice particles condensed from water vapor in the atmosphere, producing rain or snow that falls to the earth's surface.

predator an animal that lives by preying on others. Predators kill other animals for food.

relic a survivor from the past.

reptile a cold-blooded vertebrate having lungs, a bony skeleton and a body covered with scales or horny plates. Snakes, lizards, and crocodiles are examples of reptiles.

rodent any of a very large order of gnawing animals, characterized by constantly growing teeth adapted for chewing or nibbling.

salinity of or relating to the saltiness of something. The salinity of ocean water, for instance, varies in different regions and depths.

species a distinct kind, sort, variety, or class. Plant and animal species have a high degree of similarity and can generally interbreed only among themselves.

steppe a large plain having few trees.

symbiosis the living together of two kinds of organisms, especially where such an association provides benefits or advantages for both.

taiga the coniferous forests in the far northern regions of Eurasia and North America.

temperate a climate which is neither very cold nor very hot, but rather moderate.

transpiration the giving off of moisture through the surface of leaves and other parts of the plant.

tundra a treeless area between the icecap and tree line of arctic regions, having a permanently frozen subsoil.

vegetarian a person or animal that eats no meat and sometimes no animal products. Vegetarians have a diet of only vegetables, fruits, grains, and nuts.

viviparous bearing or bringing forth living young instead of laying eggs.

INDEX

CREDITS

MAPS AND DRAWINGS. G. Vaccaro, Cologna Veneta (Verona), Italy. **PHOTOGRAPHS. Archivio 2P,** Milan: 11, 28-29. **A. Borroni,** Milan: M. Mairani 32, 54, 58-59, 60-61, 102, 120-121. **A. Casdia—R. Massa,** Brugherio (Milan): 65. **Marka Graphic,** Milan: 95, 100-101. **Overseas,** Milan: A. Black 88; E. Httenmoser 50-51; Maia 47; Explorer/F. Gohier 92-93; Explorer/Suinot 90; Jacana/Bos 38-39; Jacana/A. Ducrot 12; Jacana/Ermie 68; Jacana/Massart 18-19; Jacana/Mero 52, 76; Jacana/C. Nardin 42; Jacana/A. Rainon 6-7; Jacana/J.P. Varin 48; Jacana/J.P. Varin-A. Visage 72, 84-85; Jacana/A. Visage 80-81; Oxford Scientific Films/D. Allan 37, 63; Oxford Scientific Films/S. Morris 31; Photo Credit/Ocean Images, Inc./A. Giddings 73, 74-75. **Panda Photo,** Rome: Ass. Grande Nord 27, 64, 91, cover; A. Boano 36; E. Coppola 8; S. Dimitriyevich 22, 44-45, 114-115; A. Petretti 66. **L. Pellegrini,** Milan: 10, 16-17, 34-35, 86-87, 108-109. **F. Speranza,** Milan: D. Hiser 99; D. Hiser/Aspen 83; L. Lemoine 70-71.